The State of the World Atlas

The State of the World Atlas
Michael Kidron & Ronald Segal
A Pluto Press project

Pan Books   London and Sydney

First published 1981 by Pan Books Ltd.
Cavaye Place, London SW10 9PG
and simultaneously in hardback by
Heinemann Educational Books Ltd,
22 Bedford Square, London WC1B 3HH
ISBN 0 330 26334 X

Concept and text copyright © Michael Kidron and Ronald Segal 1981
Maps copyright © Pluto Press Limited 1981

Artwork for maps created by Irene Bates, Andrea Fairbrass,
Phyllis Hoyle, Rex Nicholls, Kate Swanston, Malcolm Swanston,
Alan Turner and Ian Wakefield of Swanston & Associates,
Derby, England

Layout and other design by Marsha Austin

Editor and production coordinator: Anne Benewick

Introduction and notes typeset by Latimer Trend & Company Ltd,
Plymouth, England

Film origination by David Brin Limited, London EC1R 0JH
Printed and bound in Hong Kong by
Mandarin Offset International (HK) Limited

Contents

Introduction

The State of the World Atlas stems from the rich tradition of political atlases, born out of war or the threat of war, and out of the widespread interest that this excited in military strategy and deployment. In time the tradition came to embrace economic, social and cultural factors; reflecting and promoting the diffusion of knowledge about the world at large which has accompanied the spread of mass education, new forms of communication and international travel.

Like the others in their time, this atlas seeks to fulfil a need for information and interpretation. It identifies the major topics of public concern. It provides a frame of reference for the changing pattern of events. It explains connections that are obscure in themselves or have been deliberately obscured. And it does all this as graphically as possible, in our belief that the information so provided is more easily grasped in this way than through texts and tables.

But this atlas does rather more than its predecessors. It endeavours to be truly international: not only in showing the world-wide incidence of this or that condition or event, but in associating that incidence with an underlying structure – the self-perpetuating system of sovereign states preoccupied with aggrandisement and conflict. While it is true that the state has in its time been an instrument for the extension of personal liberty and for much material progress, it has also been an instrument of personal oppression, collective violence and economic waste. It is our contention that the destructive aspects of the state have come crucially to exceed the constructive ones.

The first section of this atlas shows how states have proliferated in the last few decades and how, with their rival claims, they are reaching out to possess the last uninhabited land mass, the high seas and the sky. The maps then turn to the military preoccupations of the state and the squandering of resources on war, the threat of war, and preparations to meet the threat of war.

The power of states rests on more than arms alone. We show how unequally states are endowed with natural and developed resources, how they employ those endowments and how they are related to the power of private industry and finance. We then consider the impact of all this on labour, on society in general and on the environment, before tracing the symptoms of crisis and identifying some of the mounting challenges to the system.

The great mass of information presented in these maps comes from governments and international agencies, whose statistics often constitute the only available source. Some states, lacking the means or the will to provide accurate statistics, may have published mere approximations – as for infant mortality rates, used in *Map 45: Bill of Health* which contain substantial ingredients of wishful thinking. In other cases, states provide no information at all, or may refuse to make public information they plainly have. The USSR and related states, for example, do not reveal figures for gold and foreign currency reserves. And in some cases, information for some states could be obtained only on a basis which would encourage misleading comparisons. In many of these, we have preferred to leave gaps.

On the understanding that all statistics may be suspect, we have used in this atlas those that we believe are valid enough for broad comparison. Band sizes have been adopted and moving averages used both to isolate certain trends and to reduce dependence on the accuracy of particular statistics. Where possible, the extreme range of statistical events has been given in the keys to the maps. And if reservations are still considered necessary, these are made in the relevant notes.

Some statistics had to be rejected altogether, a fact best exemplified by *Map 52: The Unemployment Time Bomb*, for which an International Labour Office projection was eventually used, in the form of a chart. Not only do the official unemployment rates reported by many poor states bear no recognizable relation to reality, but the existence, reported to us, of strictly confidential and alarming statistics for unemployment in advanced industrial states, confirmed our already deep suspicion of even the best figures publicly provided.

Some generally accepted statistics are marred by conceptual flaws. Gross national product (GNP) is a common measure and is used in several maps. Yet in largely agricultural societies it conveys only roughly, if at all, the value of subsistence production; and in largely industrialized societies it ignores the value of the domestic labour that confines the lives of so many women. Because it involves the use of a national currency, currently the US dollar, as an international standard, it requires further qualification. Even under conditions of monetary stability, a national currency is significantly affected by both the performance of the related national economy and by shifts in international investment. In a period of floating exchange rates, when the value of the dollar standard in other currencies moves constantly and often sharply, the distortions are enormous.

Two further observations on the use of statistics are necessary. That the very choice of which figures to collect must involve the bias of those who choose them may be exemplified by *Map 45: Bill of Health*. The provision of hospital beds is a measure of medical care that ignores traditional forms of medical treatment, available in many societies, but for which there is no statistical index. The availability of information also imposed limitations. Whereas we had hoped to include a map on the progress of the movement for women's liberation, we had to limit ourselves for lack of a more explicit measure to a comparison of abortion rights (see *Map 63: 'Our Bodies Our Selves'*).

In a number of instances, maps have been based on a degree of personal judgement. For example, information for *Map 42: The Force of Labour*, came out of intensive discussions with leading international trade union officials. Wherever possible, their judgement was checked by others. On occasion, however (for example *Map 28: Military Government* and *Map 34: Religions of Rule*), we had to fall back on our own assessment, in the light of incomplete, ambiguous or contradictory information.

Some maps, such as *Map 64: The Student Sixties* or *Map 65: Urban Heavings in the Seventies*, are the result of extensive culling of newspaper reports. And still others have been augmented in this way: *Map 32: Refugees* or *Map 44: Our Daily Bread*. Such a method presents practical limitations and had to be confined to newspapers in the major European languages.

The projection used throughout is Winkel's Tripel, an 'equal-area' projection which provides a familiar view of our spherical world. For reasons of space and scale, and because detailed information is rarely available for them, some tiny island states appear on very few maps, notably *Map 2: The Proliferation of States*, and *Map 5: The State Invades the Sea*. State boundaries conform to those used in *The Times Atlas of the World*. State names have been given on the maps in their shorter and more commonly used form: for full designations, see the list of states which follows the maps.

A project such as this could not have made the journey from concept to publication without help from many people and their resources of energy, knowledge and talent. We must, first and foremost, thank Anne Benewick, our editor, creative intermediary and production coordinator at Pluto Press. We must thank Malcolm Swanston of Swanston & Associates, who prepared the artwork for the maps, and Marsha Austin who prepared the layouts, for their keen understanding of our purposes, their inventiveness and skills. We must thank Nina Kidron of Pluto Press whose judgement and ingenuity were crucial to the publication. And we must thank Richard Kuper of Pluto Press and David Kewley of Pan Books for their continued advice and support.
   Too many people, in too many places to be listed, have responded readily to requests for guidance, information and reassurance. We are grateful to all of them. And, not least, we wish to thank each other, for mutual encouragement and understanding.

Michael Kidron
Ronald Segal
August 1980

GREENLAND

ICELAND

CANADA

NORWAY

SWEDEN

DENMARK

IRELAND UNITED KINGDOM NETH. W E

BEL. GERMANY

UNITED STATES OF AMERICA

FRANCE

ITALY YUG

PORTUGAL SPAIN

MEXICO

BAHAMAS

CUBA

JAMAICA

BELIZE
HONDURAS
GUATEMALA
EL SALVADOR
NICARAGUA

DOMINICAN
REPUBLIC
HAITI

DOMINICA

BARBADOS

TRINIDAD AND TOBAGO

COSTA RICA

PANAMA

VENEZUELA

GUYANA

SURINAM

FRENCH GUIANA

COLOMBIA

ECUADOR

PERU

BRAZIL

BOLIVIA

PARAGUAY

CHILE

URUGUAY

ARGENTINA

MOROCCO

TUNISIA

ALGERIA

MAURITANIA

MALI

NIGER

CAPE VERDE

SENEGAL

GAMBIA

GUINEA-BISSAU

GUINEA

UPPER
VOLTA

NIGERIA

SIERRA LEONE

IVORY
COAST

GHANA

TOGO

BENIN

LIBERIA

CAMEROON

EQUATORIAL GUINEA

SAO TOME

GABON

CONGO

AN

NAM

Since the world is virtually spherical it
is geometrically impossible to produce
a completely accurate world map, on
a flat sheet of paper, without some
distortion or modification.
The Mercator projection of 1569 and
the Peters Projection of 1977 display
two extremes of such distortions.
However, Winkel's 'Tripel' is used
throughout this atlas as a familiar and
relatively fair, 'equal area' projection.

Mercator's Projection 1569

Winkel's 'Tripel' Projection 1913

UNION OF SOVIET SOCIALIST REPUBLICS

MONGOLIA

TURKEY

CYPRUS
LEBANON
ISRAEL

SYRIA

IRAQ

JORDAN

KUWAIT

IRAN

AFGHANISTAN

CHINA

N
KOREA
S

JAPAN

BAHRAIN
QATAR
UAE

EGYPT

SAUDI ARABIA

OMAN

PAKISTAN

NEPAL

BHUTAN

B-
DESH

TAIWAN

HONG KONG

JDAN

N
YEMEN

S
YEMEN

DJIBOUTI

INDIA

BURMA

LAOS

VIETNAM

THAILAND

PHILIPPINES

ETHIOPIA

SOMALIA

KAM

UGANDA

KENYA

SRI LANKA

BRUNEI

KIRIBATI
(GILBERT ISLANDS)

RWANDA
BURUNDI

TANZANIA

MALAYSIA

SINGAPORE

COMOROS

INDONESIA

PAPUA
NEW GUINEA

MALAWI

MADAGASCAR

BABWE

MOZAMBIQUE

AUSTRALIA

Peters' Projection 1977

NEW ZEALAND

GREENLAND

ICELAND

CANADA

NORWAY
SWEDEN

DENMARK

IRELAND UNITED
KINGDOM

W E
GERMANY

UNITED STATES OF AMERICA

FRANCE

ITALY

YU

PORTUGAL SPAIN

TUNISIA

MOROCCO

MEXICO

BAHAMAS

CUBA

DOMINICAN
REPUBLIC

JAMAICA HAITI

BELIZE

HONDURAS

GUATEMALA

EL SALVADOR

NICARAGUA

COSTA RICA

PANAMA

VENEZUELA

COLOMBIA

ECUADOR

PERU

BRAZIL

BOLIVIA

PARAGUAY

CHILE

URUGUAY

ARGENTINA

FALKLAND ISLANDS

DOMINICAN REPUBLIC
PUERTO RICO
VIRGIN ISLANDS, BRITISH
ANTIGUA
ST. CHRISTOPHER
(KITTS)-NEVIS-ANGUILLA
GUADELOUPE
DOMINICA
MARTINIQUE
ST. LUCIA
ST. VINCENT
BARBADOS
GRENADA
TOBAGO
TRINIDAD
VENEZUELA

CAPE VERDE

ALGERIA

MAURITANIA

MALI

NIGER

SENEGAL
GAMBIA
GUINEA-BISSAU
GUINEA
SIERRA LEONE
LIBERIA

UPPER
VOLTA

IVORY
COAST

GHANA

TOGO

BENIN

NIGERIA

CAMEROON

EQUATORIAL GUINEA
SAO TOME

GABON

CONGO

A

NA

BARBADOS
TRINIDAD AND TOBAGO
GUYANA
SURINAM
FRENCH GUIANA

FRANCE

SPAIN ANDORRA

AUSTRIA

SWITZERLAND LIECHTENSTEIN

FRANCE

MONACO

ITALY

SAN MARINO

ROME

VATICAN CITY

States with a population less than Cape Town
(around 1 million)

Bahamas	Luxembourg
Bahrain	Maldives
Barbados	Malta
Botswana	Mauritius
Brunei	Nauru
Cape Verde	Oman
Comoros	Qatar
Cyprus	Reunion
Djibouti	Sao Tomé and Principe
Dominica	Seychelles
Equatorial Guinea	Solomon Islands
Fiji	St. Vincent
Gabon	Surinam
Gambia	Swaziland
Grenada	Tuvalu
Guinea-Bissau	United Arab Emirates
Guyana	Western Samoa
Iceland	
Kiribati	

2. The Proliferation of States

UNION OF SOVIET SOCIALIST REPUBLICS

TURKEY
CYPRUS
LEBANON
ISRAEL
SYRIA
IRAQ
IRAN
AFGHANISTAN
MONGOLIA
CHINA
N KOREA
S KOREA
JAPAN
EGYPT
KUWAIT
BAHRAIN
QATAR
UAE
OMAN
SAUDI ARABIA
PAKISTAN
NEPAL
BHUTAN
B-DESH
INDIA
BURMA
LAOS
TAIWAN
HONG KONG
PHILIPPINES
SUDAN
N YEMEN
S YEMEN
DJIBOUTI
ETHIOPIA
SOMALIA
ANDAMAN
THAILAND
KAM
VIETNAM
KIRIBATI
(GILBERT ISLANDS)
UGANDA
KENYA
SRI LANKA
MALDIVES
BRUNEI
MALAYSIA
SINGA-PORE
TANZANIA
COMOROS
MALAWI
ZIMBABWE
MOZAMBIQUE
MADAGASCAR
SEYCHELLES
MAURITIUS
INDONESIA
PAPUA NEW GUINEA

NAURU
SOLOMON ISLANDS
TUVALU
WESTERN SAMOA
FIJI
TONGA

AUSTRALIA

States independent before 1945

States independent since 1945

Colonies and other non-independent territories

Source: Statesman's Yearbook

NEW ZEALAND

CANADA

UNITED STATES OF AMERICA

IRELAND
UNITED KINGDOM
NETHERLANDS
DENMARK
EAST GERMANY
NORWAY
SWEDEN
FINLAND
BELGIUM
WEST GERMANY
POLAND
FRANCE
CZE
SWI
AUSTRIA
HUNGARY
ROMANIA
ALB
YUGOSLAVIA
BULGARIA

MEXICO

PORTUGAL
SPAIN
ITALY
GREECE

HAITI
DOMINICAN REPUBLIC
CUBA
PUERTO RICO
JAMAICA

GUATEMALA
HONDURAS
EL SALVADOR
NICARAGUA
COSTA RICA
PANAMA
TRINIDAD AND TOBAGO

VENEZUELA
COLOMBIA

ECUADOR
PERU
BRAZIL

BOLIVIA
PAR

CHILE
ARGENTINA
URUGUAY

TURKEY
IRAN
AF
LEBANON
SYRIA
IRAQ
KUWAIT
ISRAEL
JOR
SAUDI ARABIA
N YEMEN
S YEMEN

LIBYA
TUNISIA
MOROCCO
ALGERIA
EGYPT

MAURITANIA
MALI
NIG
CHAD
SUDAN
ETHIOPIA
SOMALIA
UPPER VOLTA
SENEGAL
GAMBIA
GUINEA
GHANA
NIGERIA
CEN
CAM
UGANDA
KENYA
SIERRA LEONE
CON
RWA
LIBERIA
IVORY COAST
TOGO
BENIN
ZAIRE
BUR
TANZANIA
(excluding ZANZIE
ZAMBIA
MALAWI
ANGOLA
BOT
ZIMBABWE
MOZAMBIQUE
LES
MADAGASCAR
SOUTH AFRICA

Average annual growth rates in population 1970-77

over 3%

2·5—3%

2·0—2·4%

1·5—1·9%

1·0—1·4%

less than 1%

population decline

data not available

States' shares of world population 1977

☐ =10 million
▫ =1 million

States with less than 1 million inhabitants excluded

AFG	AFGHANISTAN	CZE	CZECHOSLOVA
ALB	ALBANIA	JOR	JORDAN
BHU	BHUTAN	LES	LESOTHO
BOT	BOTSWANA	NIG	NIGER
BUR	BURUNDI	PAR	PARAGUAY
CAM	CAMEROON	RWA	RWANDA
CAR	CENTRAL	SIN	SINGAPORE
	AFRICAN REPUBLIC	SWI	SWITZERLAND
CON	CONGO		

Source: World Bank Atlas 1979

UNION OF SOVIET
SOCIALIST REPUBLICS

MONGOLIA

CHINA

JAPAN

NEPAL

BHU

INDIA

BANGLADESH

BURMA

THAILAND

LAOS

HONG KONG

N KOREA

TAIWAN

VIETNAM

KAMPUCHEA

S KOREA

SRI LANKA

W MALAYSIA

E MALAYSIA

SIN

PHILIPPINES

PAPUA NEW GUINEA

INDONESIA

AUSTRALIA

NEW ZEALAND

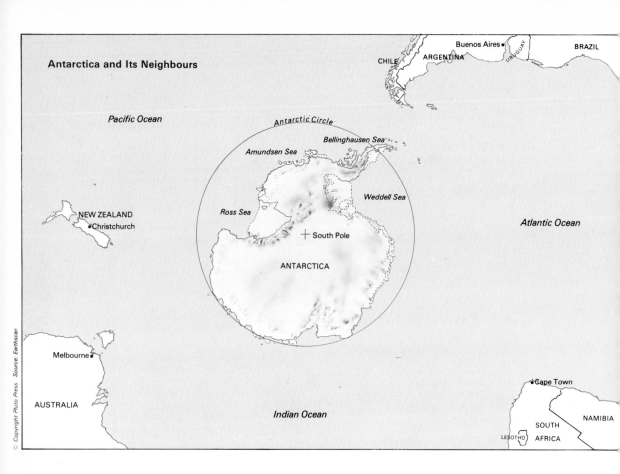

Antarctica and Its Neighbours

Pacific Ocean

Antarctic Circle

Amundsen Sea

Bellinghausen Sea

Ross Sea

Weddell Sea

NEW ZEALAND
• Christchurch

Atlantic Ocean

+ South Pole

ANTARCTICA

Melbourne •

AUSTRALIA

Indian Ocean

• Cape Town

SOUTH

NAMIBIA

LESOTHO AFRICA

CHILE ARGENTINA

• Buenos Aires

URUGUAY

BRAZIL

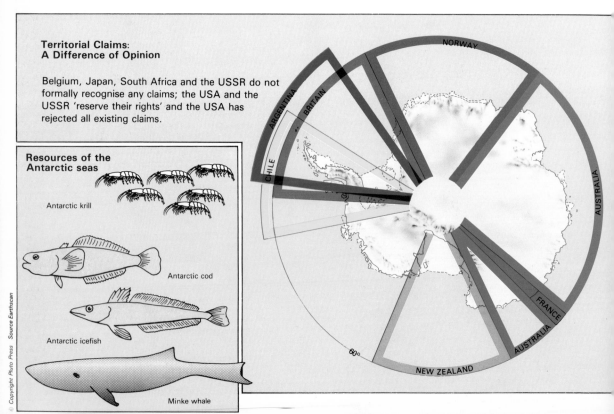

Territorial Claims:
A Difference of Opinion

Belgium, Japan, South Africa and the USSR do not
formally recognise any claims; the USA and the
USSR 'reserve their rights' and the USA has
rejected all existing claims.

Resources of the Antarctic seas

Antarctic krill

Antarctic cod

Antarctic icefish

Minke whale

NORWAY

ARGENTINA

BRITAIN

CHILE

AUSTRALIA

FRANCE

AUSTRALIA

NEW ZEALAND

60°

The Lure of Wealth

Antarctica, one hundred million years ago, showing what were until then continuous mountain ranges: the Transantarctic Mountains connected to the Andes in South America; the Central Antarctic Mountains connected to the Rand in South Africa and to mineral rich areas in Australia.

Metallic minerals already located in Antarctica include chromium (Cr), nickel (Ni), cobalt (Co), copper (Cu), gold (Au), silver (Ag), manganese (Mu), molybdenum (Mo), iron (Fe), titanium (Ti), platinum (Pt), lead (Pb), zinc (Zu), tin (Su), uranium (U). There are also vast reserves of coal and deposits of oil and natural gas: for the present, uneconomic to exploit.

□ major
□ minor

▨ historically connected mineral resources
□ located mineral deposits in Antarctica

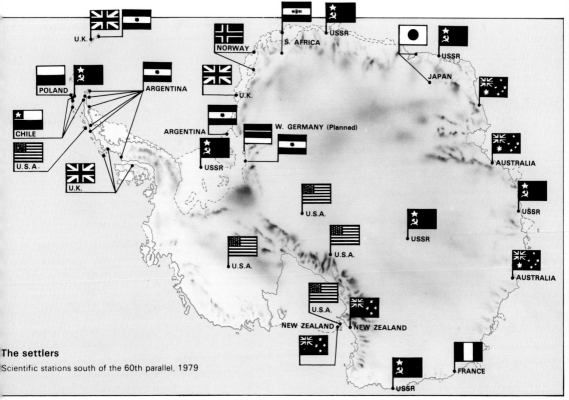

The settlers
Scientific stations south of the 60th parallel, 1979

US : Canada

US : Canada

SPITZBERGEN
Norway : USSR

GREENLAND

'Cod wars'
Iceland : UK (also W. Germany, Norway)

ICELAND

Iceland : Norway

FAROE ISLANDS

CANADA

UK : Denmark

NORWAY

SWE

see inset

UNITED KINGDOM

DENMARK

UK : Ireland

IRELAND

NETH. GERMANY

BEL W

UK : France

inset

FRANCE

CZE

AUS

Canada : France

US : Canada

US : Canada

Spain : EEC

PORTUGAL

SPAIN

ITALY

Cuba : EEC

Spain : Portugal

TUNISIA

• BERMUDA

Spain : Morocco

MOROCCO

ALGERIA

L

UNITED STATES OF AMERICA

MEXICO

BAHAMAS

CUBA

DOMINICAN REPUBLIC
PUERTO RICO

JAMAICA

BELIZE

HAITI

GUATEMALA
EL SALVADOR

HONDURAS

US : Colombia : Nicaragua

NICARAGUA

Venezuela : Colombia

COSTA RICA

PANAMA

Venezuela : Netherlands Antilles

TRINIDAD AND TOBAGO

VENEZUELA

Guyana : Venezuela

SURINAM

COLOMBIA

GUYANA

CAPE VERDE

SENEGAL

GAMBIA

GUINEA-BISSAU

GUINEA

MAURITANIA

MALI

NIGER

NIGERIA

SIERRA LEONE

LIBERIA

IVORY
COAST

GHANA

TOGO

BENIN

UPPER
VOLTA

CAMEROON

Cameroon : Nigeria

EQUATORIAL GUINEA

ECUADOR

'Tuna wars'
US : Peru

(also Canada, Japan
USSR, Greece)

(also Ecuador,
Nicaragua
Mexico, Costa Rica,
Colombia)

PERU

BRAZIL

Equatorial Guinea : Gabon

GABON

CONGO

ANG

BOLIVIA

Bolivia : Peru : Chile

CHILE

PARAGUAY

inset

NAM

URUGUAY

FRANCE

Italy : Yugoslavia

YUGOSLAVIA

⭐ Major demarcation disputes 1974-79

Major fishing disputes, 1974-79

Exclusive Economic Zones

ITALY

Albania : Yugoslavia

ALBANIA

GRE

PORTUGAL

ARGENTINA

SPAIN

Albania : Greece

Where geographically possible, most littoral
states have claimed an Exclusive Economic
Zone extending 200 nautical miles, or 350
miles or more into the continental shelf. This
map shows how an extension of national
jurisdiction to 200 miles off all coasts,
including those of islands, could affect as
much as one third of the seas that cover
70 per cent of the globe.

MALTA

Italy : Tunisia

Source: B. Buzan, A Sea of Troubles? London,
International Institute of Strategic Studies,
1978 and press reports

Chile : Argentina

MOROCCO

ALGERIA

Libya : Tunisia

UK : Argentina

FALKLAND ISLANDS

TUNISIA

LIBYA

5. The State Invades the Sea

: Norway

ay : USSR

UNION OF SOVIET SOCIALIST REPUBLICS

MONGOLIA

USSR : Japan

N. KOREA   JAPAN

N. Korea : S. Korea   S   N. Korea : S. Korea : Japan : USSR

TURKEY

YPRUS SYRIA
LEBANON
ISRAEL OR

AFGHANISTAN   CHINA

IRAQ   IRAN

Iran : Iraq
Iraq : Kuwait
Iran : UAE

KUWAIT   PAKISTAN   NEPAL   BHUTAN

QATAR   UNITED ARAB EMIRATES   B-
DESH   BURMA

GYPT

SAUDI ARABIA   OMAN

INDIA

China : Taiwan   TAIWAN

HONG KONG
China : Vietnam

N
YEMEN   S
YEMEN

India : Taiwan   Thailand : Taiwan   THAILAND   LAOS   VIETNAM   PHILIPPINES

DJIBOUTI

Thailand : Kampuchea   KAMP

UDAN

ETHIOPIA   India : Sri Lanka   Japan : India   Vietnam : Kampuchea   China : Vietnam   Thailand : Philippines

SOMALIA   SRI LANKA   USSR
S. Korea

KENYA   Somalia : Kenya   MALDIVE   Philippines : Indonesia

SEYCHELLES   MALAYSIA   Taiwan : Indonesia

TANZANIA   SINGAPORE

COMOROS   inset   INDONESIA   PAPUA
NEW
GUINEA

MALAWI   UNION OF SOVIET SOCIALIST REPUBLICS   CANADA

MOZAMBIQUE   MADAGASCAR   MONGOLIA   US : Canada

BWE   N KOREA
S   JAPAN   US : Canada   UNITED STATES OF AMERICA

CHINA

TAIWAN   US : Panama   MEXICO

Japan : US   CUBA
BELIZE
GUATEMALA   HONDURAS
EL SALVADOR   NICARAGUA
COSTA RICA   PANAMA

PHILIPPINES   France : Mexico   COLOMBIA

TURKEY   Tuvalu : Kiribati   ECUADOR

PAPUA NEW GUINEA

Greece : Turkey   INDONESIA   US : UK

CYPRUS   Papua New Guinea : Bougainville   PERU

LEBANON   NZ : US

ISRAEL   Taiwan : Australia   Solomon Is : Shortland Is   CHILE

: Egypt : Jordan : Saudi Arabia   FIJI

EGYPT   AUSTRALIA

NEW ZEALAND   ARGENTINA

One year's launching of satellites

Of the 159 satellites launched in 1978, 119 were Soviet (mainly short-lived), 30 American (longer-lived), 4 Japanese, 2 Western European, and one each Chinese, Czechoslovak, Canadian and NATO.

Of the total, probably 112 were military (91 Soviet, 19 American 1 Chinese and 1 NATO), which brought the number of military satellites ever launched to 1603, three-quarters of all artificial satellites. Over half the military satellites are for surveillance, a quarter for military communications and the rest for geodesy, navigation, early warning of attack and meteorology.

1978 saw two more Russian firsts in space: the launching of a primitive hunter-killer satellite in May, and the crash, in the Canadian Northwest, of Kosmos 945, which contaminated a large area with radioactive debris.

Tyuratam

Lop Nor

Tanegashima

tsk

Cape Kennedy ●

Vandenberg ●

Sources: COSPAR Information Bulletin SIPRI, World Armaments and Disarmaments Yearbook 1979

Foreign military presence, early 1980

army: major combat force (10,000 or above)

army: minor combat force (250 and above)

military advisors, intelligence, communications or surveillance

air force (bases or landing rights)

navy (bases or anchorage rights)

Source: A. J. Cottrell and T. H. Moore, US Overseas Bases, 1977
International Institute of Strategic Studies
Press reports

CANADA

UNITED STATES OF AMERICA

MEXICO

BERMUDA USA

BAHAMAS

USA CUBA USSR

GUATEMALA
EL SALVADOR

UK BELIZE

HONDURAS

NICARAGUA

COSTA RICA

PANAMA USA

COLOMBIA

VENEZUELA

ECUADOR

PERU

BRAZIL

BOLIVIA

PARAGUAY

CHILE

URUGUAY

ARGENTINA

DOMINICAN REPUBLIC

HAITI

JAMAICA

PUERTO RICO USA

FR. ANTILLES France

Cuba

GRENADA

BARBADOS

TRINIDAD AND TOBAGO

GUYANA

SURINAM

FRENCH GUIANA France

NORWAY

SWEDEN

DENMARK

IRELAND

UNITED KINGDOM

USA

USA

USA NETH

BELG

GERMANY WEST EAST

POLAND USSR

USSR

CZECHOSLOVAKIA

USSR

FRANCE

AUSTRIA

HUNGARY

SWITZ

YUGOSLAV

PORTUGAL

SPAIN

USA

UK

USA

ITALY

USA

ALBAN

inset

USSR

MOROCCO

USA

TUNISIA France

ALGERIA

Cuba

MAURITANIA

Morocco France

France

SENEGAL

GAMBIA

GUINEA-BISSAU Cuba

Cuba

GUINEA

SIERRA LEONE

LIBERIA

IVORY COAST France

GHANA

TOGO

BENIN

MALI

UPPER VOLTA

NIGER

NIGERIA

CAMEROON

EQUATORIAL GUINEA

GABON Cuba

CONGO

ANG

Morocco Cuba

Soe

South Africa

NAM

© Copyright Pluto Press

ICELAND

NETHERLANDS
BELGIUM
SWEDEN
NORWAY
IRELAND
DENMARK
UNITED KINGDOM
POL
WEST EAST
GERMANY
CZECH
SWITZ AUSTRIA HU
FRANCE
YUG
PORTUGAL SPAIN
ITALY
ALB

GREENLAND

CANADA

UNITED STATES OF AMERICA

TUNISI
MOROCCO

ALGERIA

MEXICO

DOMINICAN REPUBLIC
CUBA
JAMAICA
HONDURAS
GUATEMALA
MAURITANIA
MALI
NIGER
EL SALVADOR
NICARAGUA
CAPE VERDE
COSTA RICA PANAMA
BARBADOS
SENEGAL
TRINIDAD AND
TOBAGO
GUINEA
UPPER
VOLTA
VENEZUELA GUYANA
SURINAM
SIERRA LEONE
NIGERIA
COLOMBIA
BENIN
LIBERIA
IVORY GHANA
COAST
ECUADOR
EQUATORIAL CAMEROON
TOGO GUINEA
GABON
PERU
CONGO
BRAZIL

AUSTRIA JORDAN

AN

BOLIVIA

PARAGUAY

BURUNDI LEBANON SWAZILAND

NAM

CHILE

URUGUAY

FIJI MALAWI SWITZERLAND

ARGENTINA

ISRAEL RWANDA SYRIA

FALKLAND
ISLANDS

Proportion of GNP spent on military uses in 1977

- over 20%
- 2.5 - 5%
- 10.1 - 20%
- below 2.5%
- 5.1 - 10%
- data not available

Extreme range: Oman 42.7% - Mauritius 0.2%

**Proportion of central government income
spent on military uses in 1977**
where data available

50% and over

25%

10%
below
5%

Extreme range:
Equatorial Guinea 61.8% - Mauritius 0.5%

Source: USACDA World Military Expenditure and Arms Transfers 1969-77

UNION OF SOVIET SOCIALIST REPUBLICS

MONGOLIA

N KOREA

S KOREA

JAPAN

TURKEY

CYPRUS

SYRIA

IRAQ

IRAN

AFGHANISTAN

PAKISTAN

CHINA

TAIWAN

KUWAIT

SAUDI ARABIA

UAE

EGYPT

OMAN

NEPAL

BANGLADESH

INDIA

BURMA

LAOS

VIETNAM

KAM

SOUTH YEMEN

N YEMEN

SUDAN

ETHIOPIA

SOMALIA

SRI LANKA

THAILAND

MALAYSIA

PHILIPPINES

UGANDA

KENYA

SINGAPORE

INDONESIA

PAPUA NEW GUINEA

TANZANIA

COMOROS

MADAGASCAR

ZIMB

AUSTRALIA

Military Spending by Region

Europe
$232,600m

North America
$105,100m

Middle East
$26,900m

East Asia
$50,400m

South Asia
$4200m

Africa
$6100m

Oceania
$3000m

Latin America
$5900m

NATO countries
$164,700 million

Warsaw Pact countries
$163,000 million

World expenditure on
military uses in 1977
$433,900 million

Nuclear weapons delivery systems
present and planned
early 1980

hundreds   tens

ICBMs (land based
Inter-Continental Ballistic Missiles)

IRBMs
(Intermediate Range Ballistic Missiles)

SLBMs (long-range
Submarine-Launched Ballistic Missiles)

Long-range bombers with air launch
capability

Long-range cruise missiles agreed in
principle end of 1979 (US controlled)

Pershing missiles (US controlled)

Full and candidate members of the nuclear club

nuclear weapons states 'which have manufactured
and exploded a nuclear weapon or other nuclear
explosive device'

suspected nuclear weapons states 'widely reputed
to have constructed or to be able to construct
within a very few hours several nuclear weapons'

near nuclear weapons states 'now technically and
industrially able to develop the capability to
manufacture and explode a nuclear weapon or other
nuclear explosive device or will become so by
the year 2000'

states unlikely to be candidates for the nuclear
club before the year 2000

Source: Press reports
SIPRI

UNION OF SOVIET SOCIALIST REPUBLICS

TURKEY
CYPRUS SYRIA
LEBANON
IRAQ
ISRAEL
IRAN
AFGHANISTAN
KUWAIT
BAHRAIN
QATAR
U.A.E.
OMAN
SAUDI
ARABIA
N
YEMEN
S
YEMEN
PT
JDAN
ETHIOPIA
SOMALIA
UGANDA
KENYA
TANZANIA
MADAGASCAR
MALAWI
ABWE
MOZAMBIQUE

PAKISTAN
NEPAL
B
DESH
INDIA
BURMA
LAOS
SHI LANKA
KAM
VIETNAM

MONGOLIA

CHINA

2 ICBMs
in 1979

N
KOREA
S
JAPAN

TAIWAN
HONG KONG

PHILIPPINES

MALAYSIA
SINGAPORE

INDONESIA

PAPUA
NEW GUINEA

AUSTRALIA

NEW ZEALAND

ill capacity
reas of destruction: from the Hiroshima bomb to the ICBM of the mid 1980s

Hiroshima

Hiroshima

Hiroshima

Hiroshima bomb
3 sq. miles

current US ICBMs
50 sq. miles

US ICBMs for mid 1980s
290 sq. miles

CANADA

UNITED STATES OF AMERICA

MEXICO

BAHAMAS

CUBA

HAITI

DOMINICAN REPUBLIC

BELIZE

GUATEMALA

HONDURAS

EL SALVADOR

NICARAGUA

COSTA RICA

BARBADOS

TRINIDAD AND TOBAGO

VENEZUELA

GUYANA

SURINAM

FRENCH GUIANA

COLOMBIA

ECUADOR

PERU

BRAZIL

BOLIVIA

PARAGUAY

ARGENTINA

URUGUAY

CHILE

W. GERMANY

NETHERLANDS

BELGIUM

NORWAY

UNITED KINGDOM

SWEDEN

DEN

POLAND

IRELAND

E GERMANY

CZECH

AUST

H

FRANCE

YUG

ALB

ITALY

PORT

SPAIN

GREE

SWITZERLAND

TUNISIA

MOROCCO

ALGERIA

MAURITANIA

MALI

NIGER

CAPE VERDE

SENEGAL

GUINEA-BISSAU

UPPER VOLTA

NIGERIA

GUINEA

SIERRA LEONE

IVORY COAST

LIBERIA

GHANA

TOGO

BENIN

CAMEROON

GABON

CONGO

AN

NA

UNION OF SOVIET SOCIALIST REPUBLICS

MONGOLIA

TURKEY

IRAQ

IRAN

AFGHANISTAN

PAKISTAN

KUWAIT

BAHRAIN QATAR

U.A.E.

SAUDI ARABIA OMAN

N YEMEN S.YEMEN

DJIBOUTI

JDAN

ETHIOPIA SOMALIA

NEPAL

INDIA

B'DESH BURMA

SRI LANKA

CHINA

N KOREA

S

JAPAN

TAIWAN

KAM VIETNAM

THAILAND

PHILIPPINES

MALAYSIA

SINGAPORE

INDONESIA

PAPUA
NEW GUINEA

PT

inset

UGANDA

KENYA

TANZANIA

COMOROS

A

BABWE MOZAMBIQUE

MADAGASCAR

H AFRICA

inset

TURKEY

SYRIA

LEB

ISRAEL JORDAN

IRAQ

SAUDI ARABIA

AUSTRALIA

**Numbers of combat aircraft
in 1979**
(figures rounded)

100 combat aircraft

under 100 combat aircraft

Extreme range: e.g. Nicaragua 4
– USSR 6079

Source: International Institute for Strategic Studies

NEW ZEALAND

CANADA

ICELAND

UNITED STATES OF AMERICA

UNITED KINGDOM

DENMARK
NETHERLANDS
BELGIUM
LUXEMBOURG
FRANCE
E GERMANY
W GERMANY
SWITZ
AUSTRIA
PORTUGAL
SPAIN
ITALY
PO
CZEC
HUNG
YUGO
ALBANIA
GF

MEXICO
GUATEMALA
EL SALVADOR
HONDURAS
NICARAGUA
PANAMA
COLOMBIA
VENEZUELA
GUYANA
DOMINICAN REPUBLIC
CUBA

ECUADOR
PERU
BRAZIL
B P
URUGUAY
CHILE
ARGENTINA

TUNISIA
MOROCCO
ALGERIA
LIBYA
SENEGAL
G·BISSAU
G
IC
MAU
GH TO
EQUATORIAL GUINEA
GABON
CONGO

Imports into Latin America
1973-77 US $3,558 million

Imports into Africa
1973-77 US $7,738 million

Weapons exports and imports

Suppliers of world arms imports 1973-77

37.86%

12.05%
others

6.24%

5.1%

3.1%

32.81%

1.79%
1.65%

World total US $71,320 million

Shares of world arms exports/imports
depending on whether countries are
net exporters or net importers, 1973-77

☐ =1.0%

▫ =0.1%

▦ major exporters

Major arms suppliers (50% or more):

USA

W. Germany

USSR

Italy

France

China

UK

many suppliers
or data not
available

Source: US Arms Control and Disarmament Agency,
World Military Expenditures and Arms Transfers 1968-77, 1979

UNION OF SOVIET SOCIALIST REPUBLICS

JAPAN

TURKEY

SYRIA

AFGHANISTAN

PAKISTAN

MON

N KOREA

CHINA

S KOREA

TAIWAN

LEB

IRAQ

IRAN

NEPAL

BAN

BURMA

ISRAEL

JORDAN

THAILAND

KAMPUCHEA

LAOS

N VIETNAM

GYPT

KUWAIT

INDIA

QATAR

AN

SOMALIA

SAUDI ARABIA

UNITED ARAB EMIRATES

S VIETNAM

PHILIPPINES

NYA

SRI LANKA

NZANIA

N YEMEN

OMAN

MALAYSIA

A

S YEMEN

SINGAPORE

INDONESIA

PAPUA NEW GUINEA

VI

AGASCAR

AUSTRALIA

MBIQUE

NEW ZEALAND

Imports into South Asia
1973-77 US $2,417 million

Imports into East Asia
1973-77 US $11,046 million

rts into Middle East
7 US $23,767 million

CANADA

UNITED STATES OF AMERICA

USA ━━ N. Vietnam
USA ━━ Cambodia
USA ━━ Laos

MEXICO

ICELAND

NORWAY
SWEDEN
DENMARK
IRELAND UNITED KINGDOM
N W E GERMANY
B
FRANCE
S
France ━━ Libya
France ━━ Morocco
ITALY
YU
AUST

PORTUGAL SPAIN

BAHAMAS

CUBA Cuba ━━ Angola
HAITI DOMINICAN REPUBLIC
JAMAICA PUERTO RICO

GUATEMALA HONDURAS
EL SALVADOR
El Salvador ━━ Honduras
NICARAGUA
COSTA RICA
PANAMA

BARBADOS
TRINIDAD AND TOBAGO

VENEZUELA GUYANA
SURINAM

COLOMBIA

ECUADOR

PERU

BRAZIL

BOLIVIA

PARAGUAY

URUGUAY

CHILE ARGENTINA

MOROCCO TUNISIA
Morocco ━━ Algeria
Morocco ━━ France ALGERIA
L

MAURITANIA MALI NIGER

CAPE VERDE
SENEGAL
GAMBIA
GUINEA-BISSAU
GUINEA
SIERRA LEONE
IVORY
LIBERIA COAST
GHANA
TOGO
BENIN
UPPER
VOLTA
NIGERIA

CAMEROON
EQUATORIAL GUINEA

GABON
CO

Angola ━━
Af
S. Africa
NA

States at war (professional armies engaged
on both sides) at some time during the 1970s

▓▓ area of conflict

━━ ━━ states at war

Source: Press reports

© Copyright Pluto Press

12. States at War in the 1970s

UNION OF SOVIET SOCIALIST REPUBLICS

USSR ◄━► China
USSR ◄━► Afghanistan

MONGOLIA

China ◄━► USSR

N
S KOREA
S. Korea
N. Vietnam

JAPAN

CHINA

China ◄━► USSR
China ◄━► Vietnam

TURKEY

CYPRUS SYRIA

ISRAEL IRAQ

inset 1

Egypt

EGYPT

IRAN

USSR Afgh.

AFGH.

PAKISTAN

KUWAIT

BAHRAIN
QATAR
U.A.E.

OMAN

SAUDI ARABIA

NEPAL

BHUTAN

B
DESH BURMA

HONG KONG

TAIWAN

Pakistan ◄━► India

INDIA

THAILAND

VIETNAM

Saudi Arabia
N. Yemen
S. Yemen

N YEMEN

S. Yemen

KAMPU-
CHEA

PHILIPPINES

SUDAN

ETHIOPIA

SOMALIA

inset 2

Ethiopia ◄━► Somalia

SRI LANKA

MALAYSIA

SINGAPORE

UG

KENYA

Tanzania

TANZANIA

INDONESIA

PAPUA
NEW GUINEA

BIA

MALAWI

Rhodesia

NBABWE
odesia

MOZAMBIQUE

MADAGASCAR

Mozambique

COMOROS

Indonesia ◄━► Timor

inset 2

CHINA

Vietnam ◄━► China

AUSTRALIA

Australia ◄━► N. Vietnam

S

Angola

inset 1

LAOS

Turkey ◄━► Cyprus

TURKEY

Cyprus Turkey

SYRIA

Israel Leb
Israel ◄━► Syria

ISRAEL

IRAQ

Israel Jordan

Egypt Israel

SAUDI
ARABIA

THAILAND

N. Vietnam
S. Vietnam
USA
Australia
S. Korea

Laos ◄━► S. Vietnam
USA

Cambodia ◄━► Vietnam
USA

KAMPUCHEA

Cambodia ◄━► S. Vietnam

NEW ZEALAND

Antimony
World production 1976:
69,700 metric tons

Countries with 5 per cent
of more of world
production 1976:

Bolivia 21.9 per cent
China 17.2 per cent
South Africa 16.48 per cent
USSR 11 per cent

Total produced by
top four countries:
66.58 per cent

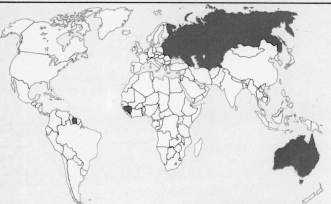

Bauxite
World production 1976:
73,800 thousand metric
tons

Countries with 5 per cent
or more of world
production 1976:

Australia 26.69 per cent
Guinea 13.9 per cent
Jamaica 14.19 per cent
Surinam 6.2 per cent
USSR 6.2 per cent

Total produced by
top five countries:
67.28 per cent

Chrome
World production 1976:
4030 thousand metric tons

Countries with 5 per cent
or more of world
production 1976:

Albania 8.4 per cent
Brazil 8.3 per cent
South Africa 26.97 per cent
Turkey 8.7 per cent
USSR 21.8 per cent
Zimbabwe 7.56 per cent

Total produced by
top six countries:
81.73 per cent

Copper
World production 1976:
8000 thousand metric tons

Countries with 5 per cent
or more of world
production 1976:

Canada 9.13 per cent
Chile 12.66 per cent
USSR 14.1 per cent
USA 18.2 per cent
Zaire 5.54 per cent
Zambia 10.62 per cent

Total produced by
top six countries:
70.25 per cent

Diamonds
(Gems and industrial diamonds combined)
World production 1976:
38,100 thousand metric carats

Countries with 5 per cent
or more of world production 1976:

Botswana   6.19 per cent
Ghana   5.99 per cent
South Africa 18.43 per cent
USSR   25.98 per cent
Zaire   31 per cent

South Africa is by far the biggest producer of gem stones

Total produced by
top five countries:
87.59 per cent

Iron Ore
World production 1976:
263,799 thousand metric tons

Countries with 5 per cent
or more of world
production 1976:

Liberia   5.3 per cent
Sweden   7.2 per cent
USSR   49.6 per cent
USA   19 per cent

Total produced by
top four countries:
81.1 per cent

Lead
World production 1976:
3330 thousand metric tons

Countries with 5 per cent
or more of world
production 1976:

Australia 11.9 per cent
Canada   7.69 per cent
Peru   5.49 per cent
USSR   14.1 per cent
USA   16.6 per cent

Total produced by
top five countries:
55.78 per cent

Manganese
World production 1976:
9840 thousand metric tons

Countries with 5 per cent
or more of world
production 1976:

Australia   7.7 per cent
Brazil   12.88 per cent
Gabon   11.11 per cent
India   6.76 per cent
South Africa 24.48 per cent
USSR   30.4 per cent

Total produced by
top six countries:
93.4 per cent

Source: *UN Statistical Yearbook 1978*

Nickel
World production 1976:
803,900 metric tons

Countries with 5 per cent
or more of world
production 1976:

Australia	10 per cent
Canada	29.5 per cent
New Caledonia (Fr colony)	14.79 per cent
USSR	19.9 per cent

Total produced by
top four countries:
74.64 per cent

Silver
World production 1976:
9690 metric tons
Countries with 5 per cent
or more of world
production 1976:

Australia	7.45 per cent
Canada	13.2 per cent
Mexico	13.68 per cent
Peru	12.13 per cent
Poland	5.15 per cent
USSR	14.13 per cent
USA	11 per cent

Total produced by
top seven countries:
76.7 per cent

Tin
World production 1976:
179,800 metric tons
Countries with 5 per cent
or more of world
production 1976:

Australia	5.78 per cent
Bolivia	16.86 per cent
Indonesia	13 per cent
Malaysia	35.26 per cent
Thailand	11.37 per cent

Total produced by
top five countries:
82.27 per cent

Zinc
World production 1976:
5520 thousand metric tons
Countries with 5 per cent
or more of world
production 1976:

Australia	8.68 per cent
Canada	17.79 per cent
Peru	8.27 per cent
USSR	13 per cent
USA	7.96 per cent

Total produced by
top five countries:
55.7 per cent

14. The World Mineral Powers

The World Mineral Powers

All countries with 5 per cent or more of at least four major minerals, 1976

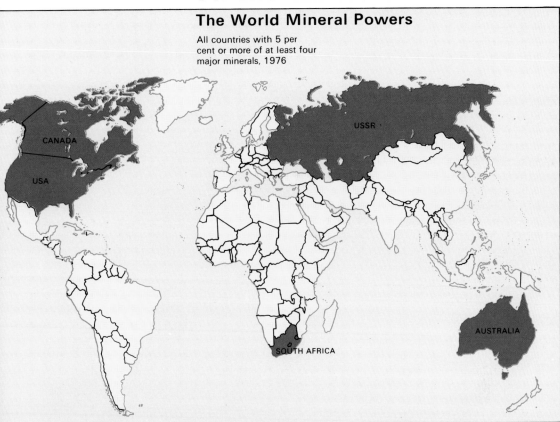

Uranium

World production 1976 (excluding USSR, Eastern Europe, China) 22,293 metric tons

Countries with 5 per cent or more of world production 1976:

Canada	21.75 per cent
France	9.25 per cent
Niger	6.54 per cent
South Africa	15.3 per cent
USA	43.95 per cent

Total produced by top five countries: 96.79 per cent

Uranium reserves

January 1978

World reserves at a market price of less than US$30 a lb. (excluding USSR, Eastern Europe, China): 1650 thousand metric tons

Countries with 5 per cent or more of world reserves:

Australia	17.5 per cent
Canada	10.12 per cent
Niger	9.69 per cent
South Africa	18.54 per cent
USA	31.69 per cent

Total produced by top five countries: 87.54 per cent

Source: *UN Statistical Yearbook 1978*

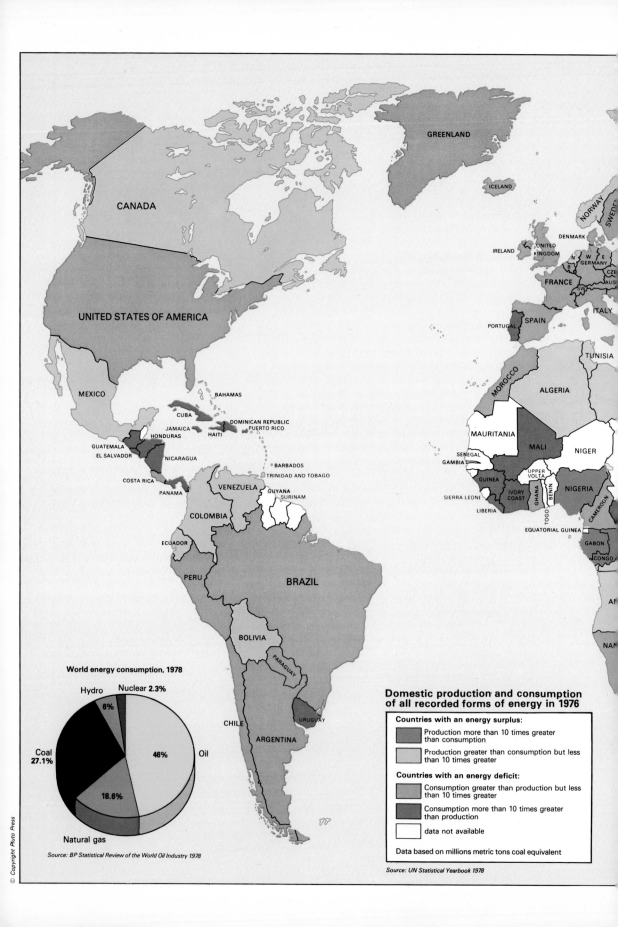

GREENLAND

ICELAND

CANADA

NORWAY

SWEDEN

DENMARK

IRELAND UNITED
KINGDOM

N W E
B GERMANY

CZE
AUS

FRANCE

SW

ITALY

UNITED STATES OF AMERICA

PORTUGAL SPAIN

TUNISIA

MOROCCO

ALGERIA

MEXICO

BAHAMAS

CUBA
JAMAICA DOMINICAN REPUBLIC
HONDURAS PUERTO RICO
HAITI

MAURITANIA

MALI

NIGER

GUATEMALA
EL SALVADOR
NICARAGUA

SENEGAL
GAMBIA

UPPER
VOLTA

BENIN

COSTA RICA

BARBADOS
TRINIDAD AND TOBAGO

GUINEA

IVORY
COAST

GHANA

TOGO

NIGERIA

PANAMA

VENEZUELA

GUYANA
SURINAM

SIERRA LEONE

LIBERIA

CAMEROON

COLOMBIA

EQUATORIAL GUINEA

ECUADOR

GABON

CONGO

PERU

BRAZIL

A

BOLIVIA

N

PARAGUAY

World energy consumption, 1978

Hydro Nuclear 2.3%
6%

CHILE

URUGUAY

Coal
27.1%

46% Oil

ARGENTINA

18.6%

Natural gas

Source: BP Statistical Review of the World Oil Industry 1978

**Domestic production and consumption
of all recorded forms of energy in 1976**

Countries with an energy surplus:

Production more than 10 times greater
than consumption

Production greater than consumption but less
than 10 times greater

Countries with an energy deficit:

Consumption greater than production but less
than 10 times greater

Consumption more than 10 times greater
than production

data not available

Data based on millions metric tons coal equivalent

Source: UN Statistical Yearbook 1978

UNION OF SOVIET SOCIALIST REPUBLICS

MONGOLIA

N KOREA
S KOREA
JAPAN

CHINA

TURKEY
PR'US
LEBANON
ISRAEL
SYRIA
JO
IRAQ
IRAN
AFGHANISTAN
KUWAIT
QATAR
UNITED ARAB EMIRATES
SAUDI ARABIA
OMAN
N YEMEN
S YEMEN
PAKISTAN
NEPAL
BHUTAN
B-DESH
INDIA
BURMA
LAOS
THAILAND
KAM
VIETNAM
TAIWAN
HONG KONG
PHILIPPINES
GYPT
UDAN
DJIBOUTI
ETHIOPIA
SOMALIA
UGANDA
KENYA
DA
NDI
TANZANIA
MALAWI
BABWE
MOZAMBIQUE
MADAGASCAR

BRUNEI
MALAYSIA
INDONESIA
PAPUA NEW GUINEA

BAHRAIN
MAURITIUS
SRI LANKA

AUSTRALIA

Coal production and consumption in 1978
Countries with annual production more
than 10 million metric tons
Source: UN World Energy Supplies 1973-78

UNITED KINGDOM
EAST GERMANY
BELGIUM
POLAND
CZECHOSLOVAKIA
HUNGARY
WEST GERMANY
ROMANIA
ITALY
USSR
BULGARIA
YUGOSLAVIA
FRANCE
CANADA
N KOREA
S KOREA
JAPAN
INDIA
SOUTH AFRICA
CHINA
AUSTRALIA
UNITED STATES OF AMERICA
NEW ZEALAND

Scale
consumption: 10 million metric tons
production: 10 million metric tons

Coal Power

consumption/production to constant scale

CANADA

UNITED
STATES OF AMERICA

MEXICO

BAHAMAS

CUBA

HAITI   DOMINICAN REPUBLIC
PUERTO RICO

GUATEMALA   JAMAICA
HONDURAS
EL SALVADOR
NICARAGUA

COSTA RICA
PANAMA   GRENADA   BARBADOS
                          TRINIDAD AND TOBAGO
        VENEZUELA   GUYANA
                    SURINAM
COLOMBIA

ECUADOR

PERU   BRAZIL

BOLIVIA

PARAGUAY

        URUGUAY
ARGENTINA
CHILE

NORWAY
SWEDEN

UNITED
KINGDOM
                    DENMARK
IRELAND

                NETH
            BEL   POLAND

                CZECHOSLOVAKIA

                    AUSTRIA   HUNGARY
            FRANCE
                            YUGOSLAVIA

PORTUGAL   SPAIN   ALBA

                ITALY

        SWITZERLAND

TUNISIA

MOROCCO   ALGERIA   LI

MAURITANIA
            MALI   NIGER

SENEGAL
GAMBIA

    GUINEA   UPPER
            VOLTA
SIERRA LEONE   IVORY   NIGERIA
            COAST GHANA BENIN
    LIBERIA   TOGO
                CAMEROON

EQUATORIAL GUINEA
                GABON
                CONGO

                        AN

                        NAM

5.85%

94.15%

Nuclear power's share of
world electricity generating
capacity 1978 5.85%

Nuclear power's share of installed
electricity generating capacity in 1978

over 15%

12.1 — 15%

9.1 — 12%

6.1 — 9%

3.1 — 6%

3% and below

no nuclear power capacity in 1978

nuclear power reactors above
20 mega-watts (E) in 1978

ten reactors

one reactor

nuclear power reactors
planned for 1984

ten reactors

one reactor

Source: SIPRI, World Armaments and Disarmament 1979
UN, World Energy Supplies 1973-78, New York 1979

UNION OF SOVIET SOCIALIST REPUBLICS

MONGOLIA

TURKEY

CYPRUS
LEBANON
ISRAEL
JORDAN

SYRIA

IRAQ

IRAN

AFGHANISTAN

CHINA

N
KOREA
S

JAPAN

KUWAIT

BAHRAIN
QATAR
U.A.E.

OMAN

PAKISTAN

NEPAL

BHUTAN

TAIWAN

GYPT

SAUDI
ARABIA

HONG KONG

SUDAN

N
YEMEN
S

DJIBOUTI

B'DESH

BURMA

INDIA

VIETNAM

ETHIOPIA

SOMALIA

THAILAND

KAM

PHILIPPINES

UGANDA

KENYA

SRI LANKA

MALAYSIA

SINGAPORE

TANZANIA

INDONESIA

PAPUA
NEW GUINEA

MADAGASCAR

ZIMBABWE

MOZAMBIQUE

AUSTRALIA

S

NEW ZEALAND

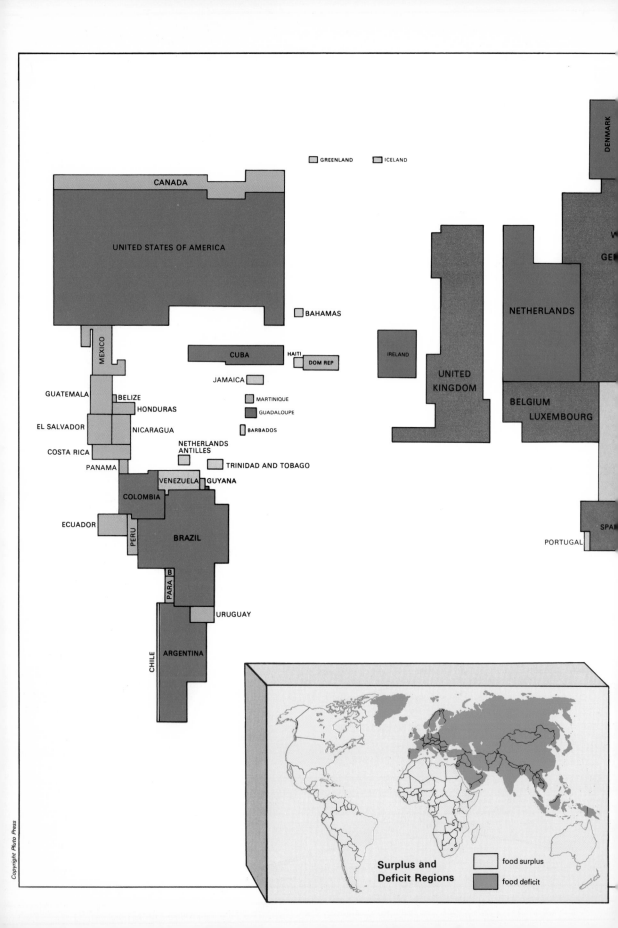

GREENLAND ICELAND

CANADA

UNITED STATES OF AMERICA

DENMARK

W
GERMANY

NETHERLANDS

BAHAMAS

MEXICO

CUBA

HAITI
DOM REP

JAMAICA

GUATEMALA

BELIZE
HONDURAS

EL SALVADOR

NICARAGUA

COSTA RICA

PANAMA

MARTINIQUE

GUADALOUPE

BARBADOS

IRELAND

UNITED
KINGDOM

BELGIUM
LUXEMBOURG

NETHERLANDS
ANTILLES

TRINIDAD AND TOBAGO

VENEZUELA GUYANA

COLOMBIA

ECUADOR

PERU

BRAZIL

PORTUGAL

SPAIN

B

PARA

URUGUAY

CHILE

ARGENTINA

Surplus and
Deficit Regions

food surplus

food deficit

Copyright Pluto Press

SWEDEN

FINLAND

EAST RMANY

POLAND

UNION OF SOVIET SOCIALIST REPUBLICS

CZECHOSLOVAKIA

AUSTRIA

HUNGARY

ROMANIA

YUGOSLAVIA

BULGARIA

ITALY

GREECE

TURKEY

IRAN

AFGH

NEP

PAKISTAN

INDIA

BANG

BURMA

CHINA

JAPAN

M

NK

LEBANON

SYRIA

IRAQ

JORDAN

ISRAEL

KUWAIT

SAUDI ARABIA

QATAR

OMAN

THAILAND

VIETNAM

L

M

HONG KONG

SOUTH KOREA

MALTA

CYPRUS

N YEMEN

SY

SRI LANKA

PHILIPPINES

TUNISIA

LIBYA

MOROCCO

ALGERIA

MU

MALI

N

B

C

CAM

EGYPT

BRUNEI

SEN

IVORY COAST

GHANA

SUDAN

ETHIOPIA

SOMALIA

MALAYSIA

SIERRA LEONE

LIBERIA

UGANDA

KENYA

SINGAPORE

RWANDA

BURUNDI

TANZANIA

MAURITIUS

INDONESIA

PAPUA NEW GUINEA

FIJI

ZAIRE

MAL AWI

MOZAMBIQUE

ZAMBIA

ANGOLA

ZIMB ABWE

NAMIBIA

MADAGASCAR

SOUTH AFRICA

AUSTRALIA

NEW ZEALAND

States with a food trade surplus

More than $1 billion

Less than $1 billion

States with a food trade deficit

More than $1 billion

Less than $1 billion

Shares of world exports or imports of world food trade, 1977 depending on whether states have a food surplus or food deficit

1.0%

0.1%

Source: FAO Trade Yearbook 1977

CANADA

UNITED STATES
OF AMERICA

MEXICO

BAHAMAS

CUBA

JAMAICA HAITI DOMINICAN REPUBLIC
PUERTO RICO

GUATEMALA HONDURAS
EL SALVADOR NICARAGUA
COSTA RICA BARBADOS
PANAMA TRINIDAD AND TOBAGO

VENEZUELA GUYANA
SURINAM

COLOMBIA

ECUADOR

PERU

BRAZIL

BOLIVIA

PARAGUAY

URUGUAY

CHILE ARGENTINA

ICELAND

WEST
GERMANY

NORWAY SWEDEN

IRELAND DENMARK
UNITED
KINGDOM GERMANY POLAND
BEL W E
CZECH
SWITZ AUSTRIA HUNGARY
PORTUGAL
YUGOSLAV
SPAIN FRANCE
ITALY ALBANIA

TUNISIA
MOROCCO
ALGERIA LI

MAURITANIA MALI NIGER

SENEGAL
GAMBIA
GUINEA UPPER
VOLTA
SIERRA LEONE BENIN NIGERIA
LIBERIA IVORY GHANA
COAST CAMEROON
TOGO EQUATORIAL
GUINEA GABON
CONGO
AN

NAM

LUXEMBOURG
MALAWI
RWANDA
SINGAPORE
SWAZILAND

**Manufacturing output
by value (US $millions) in the mid 1970s**
Where data available

each $100,000 million
figures rounded

$50,001 — under $100,000 million

$10,001 — $50,000 million

$5000 — $10,000 million

under $5000 million

Source: UN Yearbooks of Industrial Statistics, 1975, 1976, 1977

UNION OF SOVIET SOCIALIST REPUBLICS

MONGOLIA

N K

S KOREA

JAPAN

CHINA

TURKEY

CYPRUS
LEBANON
SYRIA
IRAQ
IRAN
JORDAN
KUWAIT
AFGHANISTAN
PAKISTAN
NEPAL
EL

EGYPT
SAUDI
ARABIA
QATAR
U.A.E
OMAN

N
YEMEN
S YEMEN

JDAN
ETHIOPIA
SOMALIA

UGANDA
KENYA

TANZANIA

MOZAMBIQUE
BABWE

MADAGASCAR

S

INDIA
BANGLADESH
BURMA
LAOS
VIETNAM
THAILAND
KAM

SRI LANKA

TAIWAN
HONG KONG

PHILIPPINES

MALAYSIA
SINGAPORE

W

INDONESIA

PAPUA
NEW GUINEA

AUSTRALIA

NEW ZEALAND

The Power of Persuasion

**Advertising expenditure
as a proportion of the value of industrial output in 1970**
Where data available

over 6%	4.1 – 6%	2 – 4%	below 2%

Source: UNCTAD, The Role of Trade Marks in Developing Countries, 1979.

CANADA

UNITED STATES OF AMERICA

MEXICO

BAHAMAS
CUBA
BELIZE
JAMAICA HAITI DOMINICAN REPUBLIC
GUATEMALA HONDURAS PUERTO RICO
EL SALVADOR
NICARAGUA BARBADOS
COSTA RICA TRINIDAD AND TOBAGO
PANAMA
VENEZUELA GUYANA
COLOMBIA SURINAM
ECUADOR
PERU
BRAZIL
BOLIVIA
CHILE PARAGUAY
URUGUAY
ARGENTINA

IRELAND
NORWAY SWEDEN FINLAND
DENMARK
UNITED
KINGDOM
NETHER-
LANDS
EAST POLAND
BELG- WEST GERMANY
IUM GERMANY CZECHOSLOVAKIA
FRANCE
SWITZ AUSTRIA HUNGARY
PORTUGAL YUGOSLAVIA
SPAIN ITALY
ALBANIA

TUNISIA
MOROCCO
ALGERIA
MAURITANIA MALI NIGER
SENEGAL UPPER
GAMBIA VOLTA NIGERIA
GUINEA-BISSAU GUINEA
IVORY GHANA BENIN
SIERRA LEONE COAST TOGO CAMEROON
LIBERIA
EQUATORIAL
GUINEA
GABON
CONGO

BERMUDA

CAYMAN ISLANDS

ICELAND

MALTA

MAURITIUS

SEYCHELLES

SINGAPORE

WESTERN SAMOA

**Scientists and engineers per 100,000
population in mid 1970s**

over 200

151 — 200

101 — 150

51 — 100

11 — 50

10 and below

data not available

Extreme range: USSR 488 — Honduras 0.17

*Source: UNESCO Statistical Yearbook 1977
UN Demographic Yearbooks 1976, 1977*

UNION OF SOVIET SOCIALIST REPUBLICS

MONGOLIA

TURKEY

CHINA

KOREA
N
S

JAPAN

CYPRUS
SYRIA
ISRAEL
J
IRAQ

IRAN

AFGHANISTAN

GYPT

KUWAIT
QATAR
U.A.E
OMAN

SAUDI ARABIA

N
YEMEN
S YEMEN

PAKISTAN

NEPAL

INDIA

B-
DESH

BURMA

LAOS

TAIWAN

HONG KONG

THAILAND

KAM

VIETNAM

PHILIPPINES

UDAN

ETHIOPIA

SOMALIA

SRI LANKA

UGAN
DA

KENYA

B

TANZANIA

MALAWI

MADAGASCAR

BABWE

MOZAMBIQUE

S

BRUNEI
W

MALAYSIA

INDONESIA

PAPUA
NEW GUINEA

AUSTRALIA

Brain Drain

CANADA

UNITED STATES OF AMERICA

UNITED
KINGDOM

skilled labour $11.5b

'aid' $2.3b

skilled labour $5.5b

'aid' $4.4b

skilled labour $33.9b

'aid' $39.6b

Estimated capital value of skilled immigrant labour
compared with 'development aid'
three examples, 1961-72 in US$ billions

NEW ZEALAND

Source: OECD

© Copyright Pluto Press

GREENLAND

ICELAND
fish 65% of $0.3b

FAROE ISLANDS

NORWAY

DENMARK

IRELAND UNITED KINGDOM

GERMANY
W E

N
B
L

CZE

FRANCE

AUST

ITALY

SPAIN

PORTUGAL

TUNISIA

CANADA

UNITED STATES OF AMERICA

MEXICO

sugar and honey
88% of $3.7b

CUBA

BAHAMAS
petroleum
56% of $2.5b

HAITI

JAMAICA

BELIZE

GUATEMALA
HONDURAS

EL SALVADOR

NICARAGUA

COSTA RICA

PANAMA

PUERTO RICO

TRINIDAD
AND TOBAGO
petroleum
50% of $1.8b

VENEZUELA

petroleum
66% of $9.0b

COLOMBIA

SURINAM

GUYANA

DOMINICAN
REPUBLIC
sugar and honey
63% of $0.9b

BARBADOS
sugar and honey
60% of $0.1b

sugar and honey
50% of $0.4b

MOROCCO
crude fertilisers 55% of $1.5b

ALGERIA

petroleum
85% of $4.3b

GAMBIA
oil seeds and nuts 57% of $0.05b

MAURITANIA
iron ore,
concentrates
64% of $0.2b

CAPE VERDE

SENEGAL

MALI

NIGER
non-ferrous
ores 61% of $0.09b

pe
95

GUINEA-BISSAU
oil seeds and nuts
80% of $0.006b

GUINEA

UPPER
VOLTA

BENIN

SIERRA LEONE
precious stones
60% of $0.04b

IVORY
COAST

GHANA

petroleum
93% of $8.0b

NIGERIA

CAMEROON

LIBERIA
iron ore, concentrates
75% of $0.4b

GHANA
cocoa
76% of $0.76b

GABON
petroleum
83% of $0.9b

CONGO

A

ECUADOR
petroleum 58% of $0.9b

PERU

BRAZIL

TOGO
crude fertilizers
65% of $0.1b

petroleum
73% of $0.2b

BOLIVIA

PARAGUAY

Sources of export income

<table>
<tr><td colspan="2">More than half of all export income in 1975 came from:</td></tr>
<tr><td></td><td>one product</td></tr>
<tr><td></td><td>two products</td></tr>
<tr><td></td><td>three products</td></tr>
<tr><td></td><td>four products</td></tr>
<tr><td colspan="2">More than half of all export income in 1975 came from:</td></tr>
<tr><td></td><td>fifteen products</td></tr>
<tr><td colspan="2">Less than half of all export income in 1975 came from:</td></tr>
<tr><td></td><td>fifteen products</td></tr>
<tr><td></td><td>data not available</td></tr>
</table>

DEPENDENCE

DIVERSITY

CHILE
copper ore 54% of $1.7b

URUGUAY

ARGENTINA

FIJI
sugar and honey
89% of $0.1b

HONG KONG

RWANDA
coffee 62% of $0.04b

SINGAPORE

FALKLAND ISLANDS

NAM

One product countries:
Share of total export income (in US$)
from major product is shaded

Source: UNCTAD Handbook of International Trade and Development Statistics 1979

21. Dependence and Diversity

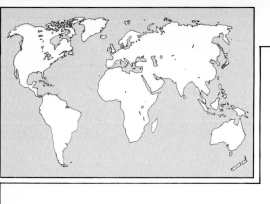

GREENLAND

ICELAND

NETHERLANDS

CANADA

UNITED STATES OF AMERICA

BELGIUM
AND
LUXEMBOURG

IRELAND

UNITED
KINGDOM

FRANCE

BAHAMAS

MEXICO

CUBA

DOMINICAN REPUBLIC

HONDURAS

HAITI

JAMAICA

GUATEMALA

NICARAGUA

EL SALVADOR

TRINIDAD AND TOBAGO

COSTA
RICA

PANAMA

COLOM

GUYANA

SURINAM

VENEZUELA

ECUADOR

BRAZIL

PERU

PORTUGAL

SPAIN

BO PA

URUGUAY

ARGENTINA

CHILE

Rate of growth or decline in export trade 1969-78

- over 100% growth
- 50.1 - 100% growth
- 25.1 - 50% growth
- 5.1 - 25% growth
- 5.1 - 25% decline
- 25.1 - 50% decline
- over 50% decline
- data not available
- 5% decline - 5% growth

Extreme range: S. Yemen 755% growth - Kampuchea 97% decline

World export trade including freight and insurance costs
1969: US$ 246,001 million   1978: US$ 1,190,400 million

States' shares of total
world exports

= 1%

= 0.1%

Source: IMF Direction of Trade Yearbooks, 1969-75, 1979

ARK

NORWAY

SWEDEN

WEST
RMANY

FINLAND

EAST
GERM

POLAND

CZECHOSLOV

ZERLAND

HUNGARY

AUSTRIA

YUGOSLAVIA

ROMANIA

UNION OF
SOVIET
SOCIALIST
REPUBLICS

BUL

TURKEY

ALBANIA

GREECE

LEBAN

CYPRUS

ITALY

ISRAEL

SYRIA

JORDAN

IRAQ

IRAN

A

PAKIST

NI

B

BAN

VIET

MON

CHINA

HONG
KONG

N KOREA

S KOREA

JAPAN

TAIWAN

INDIA

THAILAND

ALTA

EGYPT

SAUDI
ARABIA

KUWAIT

BAHRAIN

QATAR

SRI LANKA

KA

BRUNEI

MALAYSIA

PHILIPPINES

TUNISIA

UNITED
ARAB
EMIRATES

SINGAPORE

ALGERIA

LIBYA

N

S

YEMEN

OMAN

SENEGAL
GAMBIA

MOROCCO

M

JM

N C

SUD

ET

S

INDONESIA

PAPUA NEW GUINEA

GUINEA-BISSAU

GUINEA

SIERRA LEONE

LIBERIA

IVORY
COAST

GHANA

V

NIGERIA

C
R

EN

TOGO
BENIN

EQUATORIAL GUINEA

CAM

GABON

N

ANG

TANZ

MI

DJi

L

SOUTH AFRICA

MADAGASCAR

MAURITIUS

AUSTRALIA

NEW ZEALAND

CANADA

GREENLAND
ICELAND

UNITED STATES OF AMERICA

DENMARK

NETHERLANDS

BELGIUM

LUXEMBOURG

WEST GERMANY

IRELAND

UNITED KINGDOM

FRANCE

ITAL...

SPAIN

PORTUGAL

BAHAMAS

CUBA

DOMINICAN REPUBLIC

HAITI

PUERTO RICO

JAMAICA

MOROCCO
TUNISIA
ALGERIA
LIBYA
EGYPT

MAURITANIA
M
NIGER
CHAD
SUDAN
DJIBOUTI
SOMALIA

GUINEA
VOLTA
NIGERIA
E

GAMBIA
SENEGAL
SIERRA LEONE
LIBERIA
IVORY COAST
GHANA
TOGO
BENIN
GABON
CAE
CA
UG
ZAI
KENYA
TANZANIA
ZAMBIA
ZI
MALAWI
MOZAMBIQUE

MEXICO

GUATEMALA
HONDURAS
NICARAGUA

EL SALVADOR

COSTA RICA

PANAMA

COLOMBIA

ECUADOR

PERU

VENEZUELA

GUYANA
SURINAM
F GUYANA

BARBADOS

TRINIDAD AND TOBAGO

BRAZIL

B P UR

CHILE

ARGENTINA

ANGOLA
NAMIBIA

SOUTH AFRICA

MADAGASCAR
MAURITIUS
REUNION
SWAZILAND
LESOTHO

GNP per head in 1977 in US$

above $5000

$3001 - $5000

$1001 - $3000

$501 - $1000

$201 - $500

$200 and below

data not available

Extreme range:
UAE $14800 - Bangladesh $80

Source: World Bank Atlas 1979

Growth/decline in GNPs per head 1970-77

over 5% growth

3.1 - 5% growth

1.1 - 3% growth

1% growth - 1% decline

1.1 - 3% decline

over 3% decline

data not available

Extreme range: Macao 17.1% growth - Bahamas 7.2% decline

States' shares of total world GNP in 1977

= 1%

= 0·1%

CAPE VERDE
COMOROS
GRENADA
SAO TOME
SEYCHELLES

BAHRAIN
BARBADOS
CAPE VERDE
COMOROS
FIJI
F POLYNESIA
GRENADA
HONG KONG
LUXEMBOURG
MACAO
MALDIVES
MALTA
NEW CALEDONIA
QATAR

SAO TOME
SEYCHELLES
SINGAPORE

Source: World Bank Atlas 1979

People and Purses

GREENLAND

CANADA

UNITED STATES OF AMERICA

ICELAND

NORWAY   SWE

IRELAND   UNITED
          KINGDOM   DENMARK
          N   W   E
          B   GERMANY
          FRANCE   AUST
          ITALY   YUG

PORTUGAL
          SPAIN

BAHAMAS

MEXICO

CUBA
BELIZE   HAITI   DOMINICAN REPUBLIC
GUATEMALA HONDURAS   JAMAICA
EL SALVADOR
NICARAGUA
COSTA RICA   PANAMA

TRINIDAD AND TOBAGO
VENEZUELA   GUYANA
          SURI
COLOMBIA   NAM   FRENCH GUIANA

ECUADOR

PERU

BRAZIL

BOLIVIA

PARAGUAY

ARGENTINA

CHILE   URUGUAY

MOROCCO

ALGERIA

MAURITANIA   MALI
SENEGAL   NIGER
GAMBIA
GUINEA-BISSAU   VOLTA
          GUINEA   BENIN   NIGERIA
SIERRA LEONE   IVORY   GHANA
          LIBERIA COAST   CAMEROON
                                    GABON
          TOGO   CON

AN

NA

**External public debt compared with
GNPs at the end of 1977**

◼ over 80%		▨ 20.1 — 40%
▨ 60.1 — 80%		▨ 20% and below
▨ 40.1 — 60%		☐ data not available

Extreme range: Mauritania 111.56% — Nigeria 2.19%

Source: World Bank Atlas and Annual Report 1979 UN, World Statistics in Brief, 1978

**Growth/decline in external public debt
compared with GNPs between 1970 and 1977**

▲	over 200% growth	▼	0-25% decline
	101-200% growth		over 25% decline
	51 — 100% growth		*where data available*
	50% and below growth		

Extreme range: Rwanda 1559% growth — Nigeria 68.7% decline

Source: World Bank Atlas 1979 World Bank Annual Reports 1972, 1979

UNION OF SOVIET SOCIALIST REPUBLICS

MONGOLIA

CHINA

JAPAN

N KOREA

S

TURKEY

IRAN

AFGHANISTAN

IRAQ

PAKISTAN

NEPAL

BH

B DESH

BURMA

TAIWAN

GYPT

SAUDI ARABIA

U.A.E

OMAN

INDIA

VIETNAM

THAILAND

KAM

PHILIPPINES

N YEMEN

S YEMEN

UDAN

DJIBOUTI

ETHIOPIA

SOMALIA

SRI LANKA

MALAYSIA

N

UGANDA

KENYA

SINGAPORE

B

TANZANIA

COMOROS

INDONESIA

PAPUA NEW GUINEA

MALAWI

BABWE

MADAGASCAR

MOZAMBIQUE

SWAZILAND

LESOTHO

The First Bite

Payments on external debt as a proportion of export income in 1977

over 10%	2.51 — 5%
7.51 — 10%	2.5% and below
5.1 — 7.5%	data not available

Extreme range:
Mexico 48.1%
S. Yemen 0.1%

Source: World Bank Annual Report 1979

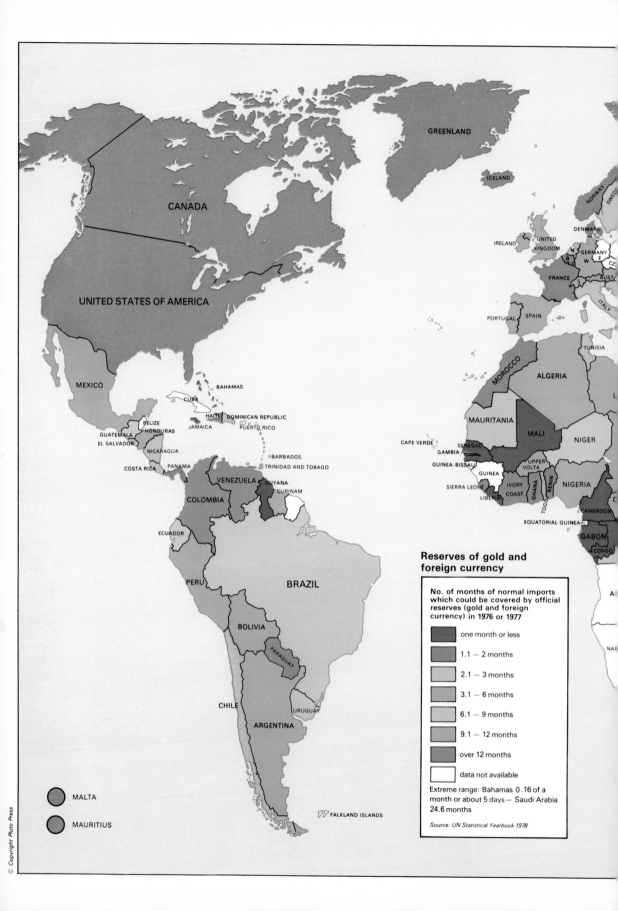

GREENLAND

ICELAND

NORWAY SWE

CANADA

DENMARK

IRELAND UNITED
KINGDOM N GERMANY
B W E CZ.
FRANCE AUST
S
ITALY

PORTUGAL SPAIN

UNITED STATES OF AMERICA

TUNISIA

MOROCCO ALGERIA

MEXICO BAHAMAS

CUBA

HAITI DOMINICAN REPUBLIC
BELIZE JAMAICA PUERTO RICO
HONDURAS
GUATEMALA
EL SALVADOR
NICARAGUA
COSTA RICA PANAMA

CAPE VERDE

MAURITANIA MALI NIGER

SENEGAL UPPER
GAMBIA VOLTA
GUINEA-BISSAU BENIN
GUINEA NIGERIA
BARBADOS SIERRA LEONE IVORY GHANA
TRINIDAD AND TOBAGO LIBERIA COAST TOGO
CAMEROON
VENEZUELA GUYANA EQUATORIAL GUINEA
SURINAM GABON
COLOMBIA CONGO

ECUADOR

Reserves of gold and foreign currency

PERU BRAZIL

No. of months of normal imports
which could be covered by official
reserves (gold and foreign
currency) in 1976 or 1977

BOLIVIA

one month or less

PARAGUAY 1.1 — 2 months

2.1 — 3 months

3.1 — 6 months

CHILE 6.1 — 9 months
URUGUAY
9.1 — 12 months

ARGENTINA over 12 months

data not available

Extreme range: Bahamas 0.16 of a
month or about 5 days — Saudi Arabia
24.6 months

MALTA *Source: UN Statistical Yearbook 1978*

MAURITIUS

FALKLAND ISLANDS

UNION OF SOVIET SOCIALIST REPUBLICS

MONGOLIA

CHINA

TURKEY
'PRUS
LEBANON
SYRIA
IRAQ
ISRAEL
JORDAN
KUWAIT
BAHRAIN
QATAR
U.A.E.
SAUDI ARABIA
OMAN
N YEMEN
S YEMEN
DJIBOUTI
ETHIOPIA
SOMALIA

IRAN

AFGHANISTAN

PAKISTAN

NEPAL
BHUTAN

B DESH

INDIA

BURMA

THAILAND
KAM
VIETNAM

N KOREA
S KOREA
JAPAN

TAIWAN

MACAO HONG KONG

PHILIPPINES

BRUNEI

MALAYSIA
SINGAPORE

INDONESIA

PAPUA
NEW GUINEA

AUSTRALIA

NEW ZEALAND

YPT
JDAN
UDA
UGANDA
KENYA
TANZANIA
MALAWI
MOZAMBIQUE
MADAGASCAR
ABWE

SRI LANKA

Imports

Imports per head 1977 US$

above $5000	$201 — $500
$3001 — $5000	$200 and below
$1001 — $3000	data not available
$501 — $1000	Extreme range: United Arab Emirates $5989.3 — Burma $9.8

Source: *World Bank Atlas 1979   UN Statistical Yearbook 1978*

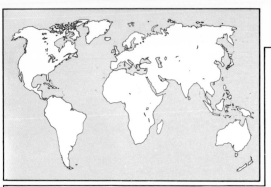

ICELAND

CANADA

UNITED STATES OF AMERICA

MEXICO

GUATEMALA
EL SALVADOR
HONDURAS
NICARAGUA
COSTA RICA
PANAMA
COLOMBIA
ECUADOR

GUYANA

TRINIDAD AND TOBAGO

JAMAICA

VENEZUELA

SURINAM

PERU

BRAZIL

B

CHILE

ARGENTINA

URUGUAY

BARBADOS

DOMINICAN
REPUBLIC
PUERTO
RICO

IRELAND

UNITED
KINGDOM

NETHERLANDS

BELGIUM

L

FRANCE

PORTUGAL

SPAIN

**Government shares of
gross domestic product**

over 25%

20 - 25%

15 - 19%

10 - 14%

below 10%

data not
available

**States' shares of total
world government
income**

= 1%

= 0·1%

*Source : UN Yearbook of National Accounts Statistics 1977
US Congress Joint Economic Committee, East European
Economies Post-Helsinki 1977 and Soviet Economy in
a New Perspective 1976*

© Copyright Pluto Press

NORWAY

SWEDEN

FINLAND

GERMANY
IST

GERMANY
EAST

POLAND

CZECHOSLOVAKIA

UNION OF SOVIET SOCIALIST REPUBLICS

SWITZ

AUSTRIA

HUN

ITALY

GREECE

TURKEY

IRAN

PAKISTAN

INDIA

BANGLADESH

THAILAND

HONG KONG

S KOREA

CYPRUS

SYRIA

LEB JOR

IRAQ

KUWAIT

SRI LANKA

KAMPUCHEA

MALAYSIA

SIN

PHILIPPINES

ISRAEL

INDONESIA

JAPAN

TUNISIA

SAUDI
ARABIA

PAPUA NEW GUINEA

FIJI

ALGERIA

MOROCCO

SEN

SL

IC

LIBYA

EGYPT

S YEMEN

OMAN

AUSTRALIA

GHANA
TOGO
BENIN

SUD

ETHIOPIA

CAM
GA
ZAIRE
KEN

NIGERIA

TANZANIA

MAURITIUS

ZAM

ZIMB

B

SOUTH
AFRICA

MADAGASCAR

NEW ZEALAND

CANADA

UNITED STATES OF AMERICA

MEXICO

BAHAMAS

CUBA

HAITI DOMINICAN REPUBLIC
PUERTO RICO
JAMAICA

GUATEMALA HONDURAS
EL SALVADOR
NICARAGUA
COSTA RICA
PANAMA

GRENADA BARBADOS
TRINIDAD AND TOBAGO

VENEZUELA GUYANA
SURINAM

COLOMBIA

ECUADOR

PERU

BRAZIL

BOLIVIA

PARAGUAY

URUGUAY

CHILE

ARGENTINA

NORWAY SWEDEN FI

DENMARK

IRELAND

UNITED
KINGDOM

GERMANY

POLAN

N
W E
B
LUX

FRANCE

SWITZ

AUSTRIA
CZECHOSLOVA

HUNGARY

YUGOSLA

PORTUGAL

SPAIN

ITALY

ALBANIA

TUNISIA

MOROCCO

ALGERIA

L

MAURITANIA

MALI

NIGER

SENEGAL
GAMBIA
GUINEA-BISSAU
GUINEA

SIERRA LEONE
LIBERIA

IVORY
COAST

UPPER
VOLTA

GHANA
TOGO
BENIN

NIGERIA

CAMEROON

EQUATORIAL GUINEA

GABON
CONGO

A

NA

Internal security forces
per 100,000 population
early 1970s

50 and below

51 — 100

101 — 200

201 — 300

301 — 500

over 500

data not available

includes some people's militia
home guard or equivalent

Source: Robert C. Sellars ed. Armed Forces of the World:
Reference Handbook, 4th ed., New York 1977
ILO Yearbook of Labour Statistics 1977

UNION OF SOVIET SOCIALIST REPUBLICS

MONGOLIA

TURKEY

CYPRUS SYRIA
LEBANON
ISRAEL

IRAQ

IRAN

AFGHANISTAN

CHINA

N
KOREA
S

JAPAN

KUWAIT

BAHRAIN
QATAR
U.A.E.

PAKISTAN

NEPAL

BHUTAN

GYPT

SAUDI
ARABIA

OMAN

INDIA

B
DESH

TAIWAN

HONG KONG

BURMA

LAOS

N
YEMEN S YEMEN

THAILAND

KAM

VIETNAM

PHILIPPINES

UDAN

ETHIOPIA

SOMALIA

SRI LANKA

PHILIPPINES

UGANDA

KENYA

MALAYSIA
SINGAPORE

TANZANIA

Workers in public administration (excluding
teachers and soldiers) as a proportion of
economically active population in the late 1970s

3 — 4%   above 6%

4.1 — 5%   data not available

5.1 — 6%

Source: Statistical yearbooks of individual countries

INDONESIA

PAPUA
NEW GUINEA

MALAWI

MOZAMBIQUE

ABWE

S

AUSTRALIA

NEW ZEALAND

GREENLAND

ICELAND

CANADA

NORWAY

SWE...

DENMARK

UNITED
IRELAND KINGDOM

GERMANY
W   E

B

CZE...

UNITED STATES OF AMERICA

FRANCE

S

AUST...

ITALY

YUC...

PORTUGAL   SPAIN

TUNISIA

MEXICO

inset

BAHAMAS

MOROCCO

ALGERIA

CUBA

HAITI DOMINICAN REPUBLIC
JAMAICA   PUERTO RICO

MAURITANIA   MALI

NIGER

GUATEMALA HONDURAS
EL SALVADOR

NICARAGUA

SENEGAL
GAMBIA
GUINEA-BISSAU

UPPER
VOLTA

BENIN

COSTA RICA

GRENADA • BARBADOS

GUINEA

TRINIDAD AND TOBAGO

SIERRA LEONE

IVORY
COAST

GHANA

NIGERIA

CAMEROON

PANAMA

VENEZUELA

LIBERIA

EQUATORIAL
GUINEA

COLOMBIA

GUYANA

SURINAM

GABON

ECUADOR

A...

PERU

BRAZIL

BOLIVIA

PARAGUAY

NAM...

ARGENTINA

URUGUAY

Continual military intervention

CHILE

CUBA

MEXICO

GUATEMALA

HONDURAS

EL SALVADOR

NICARAGUA

COSTA RICA

PANAMA

COLOMBIA

28. Military Government

UNION OF SOVIET SOCIALIST REPUBLICS

MONGOLIA

TURKEY

CYPRUS SYRIA
LEBANON
ISRAEL

IRAQ

KUWAIT

AFGHANISTAN

IRAN

CHINA

N. KOREA

S.

JAPAN

PAKISTAN

NEPAL BHUTAN

INDIA

BURMA

TAIWAN

HONG KONG

BAHRAIN
QATAR

U.A.E.

OMAN

SAUDI
ARABIA

YPT

YEMEN
N S

DAN

ETHIOPIA

SOMALIA

KENYA

RWANDA

BURUNDI

TANZANIA

COMOROS

MALAWI

BWE

MOZAMBIQUE

MADAGASCAR

SRI LANKA

BANGLADESH

THAILAND

KAM

MALAYSIA

SINGAPORE

INDONESIA

PHILIPPINES

PAPUA
NEW GUINEA

AUSTRALIA

Military rule at the end of 1978

- regimes governing by martial law
- military regimes
- regimes with substantial military participation
- all other regimes
- regime (as at the end of 1978) established by military coup
- military coup since 1960
- further military intervention since 1960

NEW ZEALAND

Source: A. S. Banks ed. Political Handbook
of the World, 1979

GREENLAND

ICELAND

IRELAND

UNITED KINGDOM

FRANCE

ITALY

PORTUGAL

SPAIN

MOROCCO

TUNISIA

ALGERIA

NIGER

MAURITANIA

MALI

UPPER VOLTA

GAMBIA

SENEGAL

GUINEA-BISSAU

GUINEA

IVORY COAST

NIGERIA

SIERRA LEONE

LIBERIA

GHANA

BENIN TOGO

CAMEROON

EQUATORIAL GUINEA

GABON

CONGO

CANADA

UNITED STATES OF AMERICA

MEXICO

CUBA

JAMAICA

HONDURAS

HAITI

DOMINICAN REPUBLIC

GUATEMALA

EL SALVADOR

NICARAGUA

PANAMA

COSTA RICA

TRINIDAD AND TOBAGO

VENEZUELA

GUYANA

COLOMBIA

ECUADOR

BRAZIL

PERU

BOLIVIA

PARAGUAY

ARGENTINA

URUGUAY

CHILE

FALKLAND ISLANDS

BAHRAIN

LUXEMBOURG

MALTA

SINGAPORE

Soldiers and teachers

Ratio between soldiers and teachers in 1974

■	more than 250 soldiers per 100 teachers
■	176-250 soldiers per 100 teachers
■	126-175 soldiers per 100 teachers
■	100-125 soldiers / teachers per 100 teachers / soldiers
■	126-175 teachers per 100 soldiers
■	176-250 teachers per 100 soldiers
■	more than 250 teachers per 100 soldiers
□	data not available

Source: Ruth L. Sivard, World Military and Social Expenditures,
Leesburg, Va., WMFE Publication, 1977

29. Bullets and Blackboards

UNION OF SOVIET SOCIALIST REPUBLICS

MONGOLIA

JAPAN

KOREA

TURKEY

see inset 1

IRAQ

AFGHANISTAN

CHINA

IRAN

KUWAIT

PAKISTAN

NEPAL

BHUTAN

TAIWAN

GYPT

SAUDI ARABIA

BURMA

N VIETNAM

LAOS

see inset 2

INDIA

BANGLADESH

THAILAND

KAM

S VIETNAM

PHILIPPINES

DAN

ETHIOPIA

SRI LANKA

SOMALIA

MALAYSIA

UGANDA

KENYA

INDONESIA

PAPUA NEW GUINEA

TANZANIA

MALAWI

BABWE

MOZAMBIQUE

MADAGASCAR

inset 1

CYPRUS

LEBANON

SYRIA

ISRAEL

JORDAN

inset 2

QATAR

UNITED ARAB EMIRATES

N YEMEN

OMAN

S YEMEN

AUSTRALIA

Soldiers

Soldiers per 1000 population in 1974

Soldier = all members of armed forces
Where data available

1 — 2.5   2.6 — 5   5.1 — 15   over 15

Extreme range: Niger 0.45 — United Arab Emirates 56

NEW ZEALAND

Military service
and conscientious objection

**Military service for men
mid 1970s**

compulsory

24 months and above

12 — 23 months

below 12 months

compulsory but selective

voluntary

reserve duty

data not available

**Conscientious objection status
early 1970s**

recognised

formally recognised
but severely restricted

not recognised

Source: International Institute of Strategic Studies
Schaffer & Weissbrodt, 'Conscientious objection to military
service as a human right', International Commission of
Jurists Review no. 9, December 1972

BAHRAIN

FIJI

UNION OF SOVIET SOCIALIST REPUBLICS

MONGOLIA

CHINA

TURKEY

RUS
LEBANON
SYRIA
IRAQ
ISRAEL JORDAN
EYPT
inset

IRAN

AFGHANISTAN

KUWAIT
BAHRAIN
QATAR
U.A.E.
SAUDI
ARABIA
OMAN

N
S YEMEN
YEMEN

SUDAN

ETHIOPIA

SOMALIA

UGANDA
KENYA
RWANDA
BURUNDI
TANZANIA

MALAWI

MOZAMBIQUE
tes
SWAZILAND
ESOTHO

ZABWE

MADAGASCAR

PAKISTAN

NEPAL
BHUTAN
B.
DESH
BURMA

INDIA

SRI LANKA

LAOS
THAILAND
VIETNAM
KAM

N KOREA
S

JAPAN

TAIWAN
HONG KONG

PHILIPPINES

MALAYSIA
SINGA-
PORE
N

INDONESIA

PAPUA
NEW GUINEA

AUSTRALIA

NEW ZEALAND

inset

TURKEY

SYRIA

CYPRUS

LEBANON

ISRAEL

JORDAN

IRAQ

SAUDI
ARABIA

inset

Capital punishment and state assassination

Prisoners per 100,000 population
1974 or nearest year

- over 150
- 101 — 150
- 51 — 100
- 50 and below
- data not available

Extreme range: USA 189 — Kampuchea 9

Source: Fifth UN Congress on the Prevention of Crime and the
Treatment of Offenders, Working Paper, 1975
Amnesty International Reports, 1977, 1978, 1979

Death penalty, as of May 1979
Where data available

- in force
- retained, but suspended in practice 1977-79
- abolished in time of peace only
- abolished for all offences

Source: Amnesty International Report, The Death Penalty
Amnesty International, The Death Penalty,
(addenda and update) 1979

CANADA

UNITED STATES OF AMERICA

MEXICO

BAHAMAS

CUBA

DOMINICAN REPUBLIC
PUERTO RICO

JAMAICA

HAITI

GUATEMALA
EL SALVADOR
HONDURAS
NICARAGUA

COSTA RICA
PANAMA

BARBADOS
TRINIDAD AND TOBAGO

VENEZUELA
GUYANA
SURINAM

COLOMBIA

ECUADOR

PERU

BRAZIL

BOLIVIA

PARAGUAY

CHILE

ARGENTINA
URUGUAY

NORWAY   SWEDEN

DENMARK

IRELAND
UNITED KINGDOM
NETHER-
LANDS
BELG-
IUM
LUXEMBOURG
GERMANY
WEST   EAST
POLA
CZECHOSLOVA
AUSTRIA   HU
FRANCE
SWITZ
ITALY
YUGOS
PORTUGAL
SPAIN
ALB

MOROCCO
TUNISIA
ALGERIA
MAURITANIA
MALI
NIGER
SENEGAL
GAMBIA
UPPER
VOLTA
GUINEA
SIERRA LEONE
IVORY
COAST
NIGERIA
LIBERIA
CAMEROON
GHANA
TOGO
EQUATORIAL
GUINEA   GABON
BENIN
CONGO
AN
NAM

31. Scourges of the State

Political prisoners and torture

Political prisoners and torture reported 1977-79
Where data available

||| political prisoners

⚡ torture widely used and officially condoned

Absence of information may only mean that the scourge in question has not been reported

inset

UNION OF SOVIET SOCIALIST REPUBL

IRELAND
UNITED KINGDOM
NETH
BEL
WEST
GERMANY
EAST
GERMANY
POLAND
CZECH
FRANCE
SWITZ
AUSTRIA
HUNGARY
ROMANIA
ITALY
YUGOSLAVIA
BULGARIA
ALBANIA
GREECE
TURKEY   *inset 1*
CYPRUS
SYRIA
LEBANON
ISRAEL
JOR
IRAQ
KUWAIT
BAHRAIN
IM

46,000 1975 —
from Vietnam

100,000 + 1976 —
from Argentina

PORTUGAL
SPAIN

120,000 + 1975
from Mozambique

420,000 + 1975

MOROCCO

82,000
1977

ALGERIA
LIBYA
EGYPT
TUNISIA

SAUDI ARABIA

MAURITANIA
MALI
NIGER
CHAD
SUDAN

1945 — 76
122,000
300,000
1975 est.

600,000
1979 est.
N
YEM
20,000
1978 est.

250,000
1977 —
DJIBOUTI
200,000
1978

CAPE VERDE
SENEGAL
GAMBIA
GUINEA-BISSAU
GUINEA
SIERRA LEONE
LIBERIA
IVORY
COAST
GHANA
TOGO
BENIN
UPPER
VOLTA
NIGERIA
CENTRAL AFRICAN
REPUBLIC

100,000
1979 est.

500,000
1977 —

ETHIOPIA
SOMALIA

1,200,000
1977 —

75,000 1976

30-35,000
1979 est.
EQUATORIAL GUINEA
CAMEROON
80,000
1979 est.
GABON
CONGO

ZAIRE

500,000
1976 est.

inset 2
25,000
UGANDA
RWANDA
BURUNDI
KENYA
265,000 1979 est.

167,000
1979 est.
TANZANIA

COMOROS
16,000
1976 — 77

UNITED STATES
OF AMERICA
CANADA

220,000 1975
from Vietnam

15,000
mid 1970's
BAHAMAS
HAITI
CUBA
DOMINICAN REPUBLIC
PUERTO RICO
MEXICO
GUATEMALA
EL SALVADOR
HOND
NIC
100,000 1979 est.
COSTA RICA
PANAMA
2,500 from
L. America
1979 est.
VENEZUELA
16,000 from L. America
1979 est. Europe
TRINIDAD AND TOBAGO
GUYANA
SURINAM

1,500
from L. America
COLOMBIA
ECUADOR
PERU
BRAZIL
BOLIVIA
PARAG

150,000 from Chile
1973 —
to Australia
New Zealand
Europe
L. America
USA

CHILE
URUGUAY

23,000
from
Europe
7,000
from
L. America
ARGENTINA

180,000
1972
700,000
1975 —
ANGOLA
ZAMBIA
NAMIBIA

58,000
1979 est.
22,000
1978 est.
MALAWI
ZIMBABWE
1,000,000 1978 est.
150,000 1978 est.
MOZAMBIQUE

MADAGASCAR

20,000
1979 est.
BOTSWANA

SWAZILAND
3,400 1979 est.

SOUTH
AFRICA
LESOTHO

MONGOLIA

CHINA

N KOREA

S KOREA

JAPAN

AFGHANISTAN

380,000
1978

PAKISTAN

11,000 *1974*

121,500 *1974*

108,750 *1974*

NEPAL

BHUTAN

BURMA

BANGLADESH

167,000
1978

250,000
1975 —

130,000
1979 only

HONG KONG

62,300
1975

TAIWAN

VIETNAM

INDIA

50,000
1979 est.

100,000

138,000
1975 —

LAOS

KAMPUCHEA

450,000 1979 est

3,500,000 1979 est.

6,300 1979 est.

140,000

PHILIPPINES

SRI LANKA

560,000
1979 est.

THAILAND

76,000 1975

MALAYSIA

SINGAPORE

40,700
1975 —

PAPUA NEW
GUINEA

INDONESIA

20,000 1975 —

AUSTRALIA

Inset 1

TURKEY

9,000
1974

CYPRUS

500,000
1979 est.

SYRIA

204,000
1979 est.

LEBANON

700,000
1979 est.

20,000
1979 est.

ISRAEL
to
strip
est.

JORDAN

IRAQ

318,000 to west bank
1979 est.

700,000 1979 est.

SAUDI ARABIA

Inset 2

UGANDA

KENYA

ZAIRE

112,000
1979 est.

RWANDA

10,000 1973

BURUNDI

40,000 1973

500,000
1973

TANZANIA

Numbers of new refugees 1972-79
including residual Palestinian refugee population

→ over 300,000

→ 150,000 — 300,000

→ 50,000 — 150,000

→ below 50,000

↻ population internally displaced 1972-79

Source: Minority Rights Group
Keesings Contemporary Archives
Press reports

NEW ZEALAND

CANADA ★

UNITED STATES OF AMERICA

MEXICO

BAHAMAS E
CUBA
S JAMAICA   DOMINICAN REPUBLIC
BELIZE   HAITI PUERTO RICO E
GUATEMALA HONDURAS   F
EL SALVADOR
NICARAGUA
COSTA RICA   BARBADOS E
PANAMA   TRINIDAD AND TOBAGO E

VENEZUELA
GUYANA
COLOMBIA E SURINAM
         D F FRENCH GUIANA

ECUADOR S

PERU S
            BRAZIL

BOLIVIA S
        S PARAGUAY
CHILE

URUGUAY

ARGENTINA

FALKLAND ISLANDS

NORWAY
SWEDEN
DENMARK
IRELAND UNITED ★
KINGDOM NETHERLANDS EAST POLAN
         BELGIUM   WEST GERMANY
                    GERMANY CZECHOSLOVAKIA
         FRANCE   SWITZ ★ AUSTRIA HUNG
                    ITALY   YUGOSLA
         S
PORTUGAL S   ALB
SPAIN S
    ★   I

TUNISIA
    F
MOROCCO ALGERIA
         ★
                MAURITANIA MALI NIGER
P CAPE VERDE   F   F   F
          SENEGAL
       E GAMBIA   UPPER
P GUINEA-BISSAU   VOLTA
         GUINEA F F   NIGERIA
E SIERRA LEONE IVORY GHANA BENIN E E/F
         COAST
   E LIBERIA   F F F CAMEROON
                TOGO
               S EQUATORIAL GUINEA
                P SAO TOME   GABON
                              CONGO F
                                    A

                              NA
                              Af

E FIJI
F E MAURITIUS
E/F SEYCHELLES
E WESTERN SAMOA

Official language or languages

- not the languages of the majority
- spoken by the majority but not by many of the poor
- spoken by most people in creole form
- widely spoken throughout country or in appropriate region

⬡ old imperial language or languages, not official, but still used in government and business

★ countries with significant linguistic conflict

© Copyright Pluto Press

A language of rule is one which is used by the governing classes, and which helps to secure their dominance

UNION OF SOVIET SOCIALIST REPUBLICS

MONGOLIA

N KOREA

S KOREA

JAPAN

R

inset
TURKEY
Fa
SYRIA

IRAN
Fa

IRAQ

KUWAIT

AFGHANISTAN

PAKISTAN

QATAR

UAE

SAUDI ARABIA

OMAN

N YEMEN

S YEMEN

DJIBOUTI

NEPAL

B DESH

BURMA

THAILAND

LAOS

KAM

VIETNAM

CHINA
Pu

TAIWAN

HONG KONG E

MACAO P

PHILIPPINES

T E/S

BRUNEI

MALAYSIA

E SINGAPORE

In INDONESIA

PAPUA NEW GUINEA
E

INDIA
H/E

JDAN

ETHIOPIA
Am

SOMALIA

KENYA
Sw

UGANDA E

RWANDA F

BURUNDI F

MALAWI E

COMOROS F

TANZANIA

MOZAMBIQUE
P

MADAGASCAR

BABWE
E

SWAZILAND E

LESOTHO E

/E

inset

CYPRUS

SYRIA

LEBANON
F/E

ISRAEL
Heb

JORDAN

SRI LANKA

MALAYSIA

AUSTRALIA

NEW ZEALAND

Languages

Afrikaans	**Af**	Bahasa Indonesia	**In**
Amharic	**Am**	Irish Gaelic	**Ir**
Arabic	**A**	Italian	**I**
Dutch	**D**	Portuguese	**P**
English	**E**	Putonghua	**Pu**
Farsi	**Fa**	Russian	**R**
French	**F**	Spanish	**S**
German	**G**	Swahili	**Sw**
Hebrew	**Heb**	Tagalog	**T**
Hindi	**H**	Urdu	**U**

Source: Europa Yearbook 1978
Statesman's Yearbook 1977, 1978, 1979,
US. CIA National Basic Intelligence Factbook
Private sources

CANADA

UNITED STATES OF AMERICA

MEXICO

BAHAMAS

CUBA
JAMAICA
HONDURAS
GUATEMALA
EL SALVADOR
NICARAGUA
COSTA RICA
PANAMA

DOMINICAN REPUBLIC
PUERTO RICO
HAITI

TRINIDAD AND TOBAGO

VENEZUELA
GUYANA
SURINAM
FRENCH GUIANA

COLOMBIA

ECUADOR

PERU

BRAZIL

BOLIVIA

PARAGUAY

CHILE

URUGUAY

ARGENTINA

BAHRAIN

BARBADOS

BRUNEI

FIJI

ICELAND

MALTA

MAURITIUS

REUNION

WESTERN SAMOA

NORWAY
SWEDEN
FINLA

DENMARK

IRELAND
UNITED
KINGDOM

NETH
BELG
WEST
GERMANY
EAST
POLAND
LUXEMBOURG
CZECHOSLOVAKIA
FRANCE
SWITZ
AUSTRIA
HUNGARY
RO
ITALY
YUGOSLAVIA
PORTUGAL
SPAIN
Rome
ALBANIA
GRE

TUNISIA

MOROCCO
ALGERIA
LI

MAURITANIA
MALI
NIGER

SENEGAL
GAMBIA
GUINEA-BISSAU
GUINEA
SIERRA LEONE
LIBERIA
IVORY
COAST
UPPER
VOLTA
GHANA
BENIN
TOGO
NIGERIA

CAMEROON

EQUATORIAL
GUINEA
GABON
CONGO

AF

NAM

Source: Europa, Middle East and North Africa Yearbook 1979-80
Europa, Africa South of the Sahara Yearbook 1978-79
Europa, The Far East and Australasia Yearbook 1978-79
C. Veliz (ed). Latin America and the Caribbean: a Handbook, 1968
Statistical Yearbook of the Netherlands, 1978
Private sources

Animism

Buddhism

Shintoism

Christianity

Christianity
(no dominant sect)

Catholicism

Protestantism

other Christianity
(Orthodox, Maronite etc.)

Hinduism

Islam

Sunni

Shi'ism and sub-sects

Judaism

Marxism-Leninism

Moscow denomination

Peking denomination

Moscow alignment

local variant

■ Holy capitals

★ site of recent
religious conflict

© Copyright Pluto Press

A religion of rule is one which is professed by the governing classes and which sustains their solidarity

Big money

National reserves compared with assets of banks at the end of 1976

reserves below Bank of America, but above National Westminster Bank ($29,080 million) the 20th in size

reserves below National Westminster, but above Hong Kong & Shanghai Banking Corporation ($14,188 million) the 75th in size

reserves below Hong Kong & Shanghai Banking Corporation, but above Bank of Hiroshima ($4,822 million) the 150th in size

reserves below Bank of Hiroshima but above Cantonal Bank of St. Gall ($1,707 million) the 300th in size

reserves below Cantonal Bank of St. Gall

data not available

No state has reserves above the assets of The Bank of America ($73,913 million), the world's largest bank.

NEW ZEALAND

AUSTRALIA

PAPUA NEW GUINEA

KOREA S

JAPAN

TAIWAN

PHILIPPINES

INDONESIA

VIETNAM

C'AM

THAILAND

MALAYSIA

BURMA

MONGOLIA

CHINA

UNION OF SOVIET SOCIALIST REPUBLICS

B'DESH

NEPAL

INDIA

SRI LANKA

PAKISTAN

AFGH

IRAN

KUWAIT

IRAQ

SY

OMAN

SAUDI ARABIA

N YEM S YEMEN

SOMALIA

MADAGASCAR

TURKEY

CYPRUS

GREECE

BUL

ROM

YUGO

HUN

AUT

ITALY

FRANCE

POL

W GER

E GER

DEN

FINLAND

SWEDEN

NORWAY

IRELAND

UNITED KINGDOM

SPAIN

PORTUGAL

MOROCCO

ALGERIA

TUNISIA

LIBYA

EGYPT

SUDAN

ETHIOPIA

UG

KENYA

TANZ

MOZAMBIQUE

ZAIRE

C A R

CHAD

NIGER

MALI

MAURITANIA

SENEGAL

GAMBIA

GUINEA-BISSAU

GUINEA

SIERRA LEONE

LIBERIA

IVORY CO

GHANA

VOLTA

TOGO

BENIN

NIGERIA

CAM

GABON

CO

ANGOLA

ZAMBIA

ZIMB

NAMIBIA

BOTS

SOUTH AFRICA

ICELAND

GREENLAND

CANADA

UNITED STATES OF AMERICA

MEXICO

GUATEMALA

BELIZE

EL SALVADOR

HONDURAS

NICARAGUA

COSTA RICA

PANAMA

BAHAMAS

CUBA

JAMAICA

HAITI

DOMINICAN REPUBLIC

TRINIDAD AND TOBAGO

VENEZUELA

COLOMBIA

GUYANA

SURINAM

ECUADOR

PERU

BRAZIL

BOLIVIA

PARAG

CHILE

ARGENTINA

URUGUAY

FALKLAND ISLANDS

Source:
International Financial Statistics 1977
The Banker, July 1977

Big business

National incomes (1977 GNPs) compared with sales incomes of US multinationals in 1977

GNP greater than income of Exxon, but above that of Mobil ($26.062 billion) the 5th in size

GPN below income of Mobil, but above that of Chrysler ($11.7 billion) the 10th in size

GNP below income of Chrysler, but above that of Coca Cola ($2.87 billion) the 64th in size

GNP below income of Coca Cola, but above that of Time Inc. ($0.91 billion) the 221st in size

GNP below that of Time Inc.

data not available

Source:
World Bank Atlas 1977
Fortune, May 1977

CANADA

UNITED STATES OF AMERICA

MEXICO

BAHAMAS

CUBA
JAMAICA HAITI DOMINICAN REPUBLIC
PUERTO RICO

GUATEMALA HONDURAS
EL SALVADOR
NICARAGUA
NETHERLANDS ANTILLES
BARBADOS
COSTA RICA
TRINIDAD AND TOBAGO
PANAMA

VENEZUELA
GUYANA
SURINAM
COLOMBIA

ECUADOR

PERU

BRAZIL

BOLIVIA

PARAGUAY

CHILE

URUGUAY

ARGENTINA

**Transnationals with sales of
more than US $1 billion
at the end of 1976**

■▶ $1b – 1.99b

▣▶ $2b – 3.99b

▣▶ $4b – 5.99b

▣▶ $6b – 7.99b

▉ $8 billion and over

Source: UN Centre on Transnational Corporations,
Transnational Corporations in World Development,
UNESCO 1978

NORWAY

IRELAND
DENMARK
WEST
GERMANY
NETHERLANDS
UNITED KINGDOM
SW
BELGIUM
EAST
GERMAN

FRANCE
SWITZ
A

PORTUGAL
ITALY

SPAIN

MOROCCO

ALGERIA

MAURITANIA
MALI
NIGER

SENEGAL
GAMBIA
UPPER
VOLTA
GUINEA
NIGERIA
SIERRA LEONE
IVORY
COAST
GHANA
BENIN
LIBERIA
TOGO
CAMEROON

Source: UN Centre on Transnational Corporations,
Transnational Corporations in World Development,
UNESCO 1978

UNION OF SOVIET SOCIALIST REPUBLICS

MONGOLIA

CHINA

TURKEY

SYRIA

IRAQ

IRAN

AFGHANISTAN

ISRAEL

JORDAN

KUWAIT

PAKISTAN

NEPAL

BHU

QATAR

UAE

SAUDI ARABIA

OMAN

INDIA

BANGLADESH

BURMA

N YEMEN

S YEMEN

LAOS

VIETNAM

THAILAND

ETHIOPIA

SOMALIA

SRI LANKA

KAM

N KOREA

S

KOREA

JAPAN

TAIWAN

PHILIPPINES

MALAYSIA

INDONESIA

PAPUA NEW GUINEA

AUSTRALIA

The Drug Trade

Ownership of the pharmaceutical industry
Estimate of foreign control
Selected countries 1975 or nearest year

25% and below	50.1 — 75%
25.1 — 50%	75.1 — 100%

Extreme range: United States 15% —
Saudi Arabia 100%

NAMIBIA

BOTSWANA

SW

SOUTH AFRICA

NEW ZEALAND

TURKEY

LEBANON
SYRIA
ISRAEL JORDAN
IRAN

BAHRAIN
U.A.E. **t**
S.YEMEN

INDIA

S KOREA

UNITED S

TAIWAN
MEXIC

T MACAO HONG KONG
Hong Kong 13

THAILAND

PHILIPPINES

GU
EL

Hong

T
MALDIVE

SRI LANKA

T BRUNEI
MALAYSIA

SINGAPORE

INDONESIA

W. German 145

Japan 75

Switzerland 53   Hong Kong 28

UK 31   Greece 17   Norway 12

W. G

◯MAURITIUS

NETHERLANDS ANTILLES

NICARAGUA

JAMAICA

HAITI

PUERTO RICO

Tax havens and Flags of convenience

tax havens

■ major

■ minor

flags of convenience, 1978
beneficial owners registered in
country of harbour
(owners of 10 or more vessels only)

T	no taxation (or virtually none)
t	low taxation
S	strict banking secrecy
🏭	tax benefits for companies
🏭	tax benefits for shipping companies
👤	tax benefits for certain people

ISLE OF MAN

UNITED
KINGDOM

LUXEMBOURG

GUERNSEY
JERSEY

SWITZERLAND   LIECHTENSTEIN

MONACO

ANDORRA

GREECE

Greece 475

W. Germany 52

MALTA

CYPRUS

TUNISIA

MOROCCO

EGYPT

BERMUDA

Canada 47   USA 11

BAHAMAS

USA 11

TURKS AND CAICOS

CAYMAN

HAITI DOMINICAN REPUBLIC
VIRGIN ISLANDS
ANGUILLA

JAMAICA   PUERTO
RICO   ANTIGUA

ST LUCIA
BARBADOS
NETH   GRENADA
ANTILLES   TRINIDAD
AND TOBAGO

HURAS

RAGUA

PANAMA

VENEZUELA

COLOMBIA

SENEGAL

IVORY
COAST   GHANA

LIBERIA

USA 576

Greece 571

H. Kong 550   Norway 38

Japan 168   Israel 37

W. Germany 72   Italy 37

Switz. 84   Neths 30   Canada 14

UK 53   Monaco 23   N. Korea 14

JADOR

RU

BRAZIL

HEBRIDES

BOTSWANA

SWAZILAND

LESOTHO

SOUTH AFRICA

CHILE

URUGUAY

RN SAMOA

Production zones

free production zones

● major

● minor

offshore manufacturing zones

■ major

▱ minor

▱ under construction 1975

Sources:
UNCTAD, Handbook of International Trade
and Development Statistics, 1979
B. Spitz, Tax Havens Encyclopedia, 1978
Froebel, Heinrichs & Kreye,
The New International Division of Labour, 1980
Private sources

CANADA

UNITED STATES OF AMERICA

+3%

3,000,000

MEXICO

NORWAY

**Total numbers of foreign workers
in the mid 1970s**

arrivals   departures

below 100,000

100,000 — 200,000

200,000 — 300,000

300,000 — 400,000

400,000 — 600,000

over 600,000

total
28,000   DEN

others
948,000

total
76,000

IRELAND

→ UK

→ others

UNITED
KINGDOM

+7%

Ireland

452,000

Spain
37,000

Italy
72,000

Greece
50,000

NETHERLANDS

+4.7%

Spain
34,000

others

BELGIUM

+7.1%

others
36,000
total

L 26,400

W
GER

+

Morocco
30,000

Italy
90,000

Portugal
85,000

Spain
165,000

Morocco
16,000

FRANCE

+11%

SWITZER-
LAND

others
176,000

Italy
230,000

Yugoslavia
50,000

SPAIN -4.7%

Portugal
475,000

Spain
265,000

Morocco
130,000

Tunisia
70,000

Algeria
440,000

PORTUGAL

-14.2%

→ Belgium

→ W. Germany

→ France

→ UK

→ Switzerland

→ others

→ W. Germany

→ France

→ others

Countries of labour immigration

Countries of labour emigration

Worker migrants as a proportion of:

the host (+) country's labour force

the home (−) country's labour force

MOROCCO

↑ Belgium

↑ France

↑ others

ALGERIA

↑ France

↑ others

TU

W

Source: Minority Rights Group 1978
Government statistical yearbooks
UN, World Population Trends and Policies, 1977
Private sources

SWEDEN

Finland
187,600

UNION OF SOVIET
SOCIALIST REPUBLICS

40,000

EAST
GERMANY

POLAND

others

Yugoslavia

Turkey

CZECHOSLOVAKIA

590,000

Greece

AUSTRIA

225,000
to Switzerland

32,000

HUNGARY

ROMANIA

YUGOSLAVIA -8.5%

others France

W. Germany Sweden

BULGARIA

6%

W.Germany

France

UK

total
26,000

Switzerland

others

ALBANIA

GREECE -7.8%

W. Germany

UK

others

MAURITANIA

+16%

SENEGAL

GAMBIA

GUINEA-
BISSAU

150,000

GUINEA

SIERRA LEONE

LIBERIA

MALI

1,400,000 from U. Volta,
Mali, Guinea, Niger

NIGER

IVORY
COAST +55%

GHANA

+24%

TOGO

BENIN

NIGERIA

900,000 from
Togo,
U. Volta, others

CAMEROON

NAMIBIA

BOTSWANA

-12%

MALAWI -3.5%

34,000

138,000 10,000

SOUTH AFRICA

+5%

79,000

MOZAMBIQUE

-4.5%

-8%

SWAZILAND

129,000

from Mozambique

LESOTHO -29%

TURKEY -4.5%

W. Germany

others

LIBYA

+22%

EGYPT

118,000

SUDAN

LIBYA

SYRIA

LEBANON

ISRAEL

JORDAN

IRAQ

KUWAIT
+80%

IRAN

213,000

343,000

22,400

400

QATAR

BAHRAIN

SAUDI ARABIA

+50%

UNITED
ARAB
EMIRATES +88%

OMAN

748,000

N YEMEN

S YEMEN

ETHIOPIA

SOMALIA

India

Bangladesh

Pakistan

S. Korea

Afghanistan

+37% Bahrain

+88% Qatar

ICELAND

NETHERLANDS
BELGIUM

NORWAY

SWEDEN

IRELAND

UNITED
KINGDOM

DENMARK

LUXEMBOURG

GERMANY
WEST   EAST

POLAND

FRANCE

SWITZ

AUS

CZECH

HUNGARY

PORTUGAL

SPAIN

ITALY

YUGOSLAV

ALB

GREENLAND

CANADA

UNITED STATES OF AMERICA

BAHAMAS

MEXICO

CUBA

DOMINICAN REPUBLIC

JAMAICA

HAITI

BELIZE

GUATEMALA
EL SALVADOR

HONDURAS

NICARAGUA

BARBADOS

COSTA RICA

TRINIDAD AND TOBAGO

PANAMA

VENEZUELA

GUYANA

SURINAM

COLOMBIA

ECUADOR

PERU

BRAZIL

BOLIVIA

PARAGUAY

ARGENTINA

URUGUAY

CHILE

FALKLAND ISLANDS

TUNISIA

MOROCCO

ALGERIA

L

MAURITANIA

MALI

NIGER

SENEGAL

GUINEA

UPPER
VOLTA

NIGERIA

SIERRA LEONE

BENIN

LIBERIA

CAMEROON

IVORY
COAST

TOGO

GABON

CONGO

GHANA

A

NA

© Copyright Pluto Press

UNION OF SOVIET SOCIALIST REPUBLICS

MONGOLIA

N KOREA

S KOREA

JAPAN

CHINA

TURKEY
inset

SYRIA

IRAQ

IRAN

AFGHANISTAN

PAKISTAN

NEPAL

SAUDI ARABIA

OMAN

KUWAIT

INDIA

BANGLADESH

BURMA

LAOS

HONG KONG

VIETNAM

PHILIPPINES

YPT

N YEM

S YEMEN

KAM

ETHIOPIA

SOMALIA

SRI LANKA

THAILAND

MALAYSIA

UGANDA

KENYA

TANZANIA

MALAWI

SINGAPORE

INDONESIA

PAPUA NEW GUINEA

ZIMB

MOZAMBIQUE

MADAGASCAR

inset

TURKEY

CYPRUS

LEBANON

SYRIA

IRAQ

ISRAEL

JORDAN

SAUDI
ARABIA

SWAZILAND

AUSTRALIA

Levels of exploitation in manufacturing, 1970s

1st level   2nd level   3rd level   4th level   5th level
Where data available

Exploitation for this purpose is defined as:
gross output in manufacturing minus payroll in manufacturing
divided by payroll in manufacturing

NEW
ZEALAND

Source: UN Yearbooks of Industrial Statistics, 1978 and 1979 Vol. 1

Workers on the land

Proportion of economically active labour force
in agriculture in mid 1970s

- over 60%
- 50.1 — 60%
- 40.1 — 50%
- 30.1 — 40%
- 20.1 — 30%
- 10.1 — 20%
- 10% and below
- data not available

Extreme range: 94.4% Nepal — 2.19% Singapore

BAHRAIN
BARBADOS
FIJI
HONG KONG
LUXEMBOURG
MALTA
MAURITIUS
SINGAPORE
SEYCHELLES
WESTERN SAMOA

Source:
I.L.O. Yearbook of Labour Statistics, 1979
I.L.O. Statistical Yearbook, 1977, 1978
UN, Statistical Yearbook, 1976
UN, Statistical Yearbook for Asia and the Pacific, 1977

Workers in industry

Proportion of economically active labour force in mining,manufacturing and transport in mid 1970s

over 40%
30.1 — 40%
20.1 — 30%
10.1 — 20%
10% and below
data not available

Extreme range: 51.8% Hong Kong — 1.3% Nepal

BARBADOS
FIJI
HONG KONG
LUXEMBOURG
MAURITIUS
SEYCHELLES
SINGAPORE
WESTERN SAMOA

Source:
I.L.O. Yearbook of Labour Statistics, 1979
I.L.O. Statistical Yearbook, 1977, 1978
UN, Statistical Yearbook, 1976
UN, Statistical Yearbook for Asia and the Pacific, 1977

CANADA 28

UNITED STATES OF AMERICA
13

ICELAND
61

NORWAY
52   SWEDEN
27

IRELAND
66   UNITED
KINGDOM
8   DENMARK
NETH
38   GERMANY
BEL   WEST   EAST
16   POLAND
65
LUXEMBOURG   CZECH
46   40+   AUST
FRANCE   SWITZ   3
40+   HUNG
MONACO   62   2
31   47   YUG
ITALY   78
PORTUGAL   SPAIN   ALBANIA
48   58   9   4
TUNISIA   MALTA

BAHAMAS 17

MEXICO
30   CUBA 60
18   DOMINICAN REPUBLIC
JAMAICA   PUERTO RICO
GUATEMALA   79   HAITI   20
53   HONDURAS   74
EL SALVADOR   21   NICARAGUA
15   7   BARBADOS
COSTA RICA   GRENADA   TRINIDAD AND TOBAGO   11
68   PANAMA   VENEZUELA   14
81   54   GUYANA   49
COLOMBIA   SURINAM
56
ECUADOR   42
PERU   35
24   BRAZIL
82
BOLIVIA
6
PARAGUAY
10   36   URUGUAY
CHILE   ARGENTINA   25

MOROCCO   ALGERIA
69   44
MAURITANIA   MALI   NIGER
SENEGAL
GAMBIA   UPPER
GUINEA-BISSAU   GUINEA   VOLTA
91   SIERRA LEONE   NIGERIA
92   LIBERIA   IVORY   GHANA   BENIN
COAST   72   CAMEROON
EQUATORIAL GUINEA   77
GABON   CONGO

FIJI

45   WESTERN SAMOA

Sexual discrimination in jobs
5 Countries ranked from Bulgaria 1 (least discrimination) to Syria 94 (most discrimination) in 1976
Where data available

Index: the proportion of women (or men) who would have to change their occupational or industrial classification for there to be sex equality in jobs

Source: Elise Boulding et al, Handbook of International Data on Women 1976

Women as a proportion of the non-domestic labour force: latest year between 1975 and 1979

over 40%

30.1 - 40%

20.1 - 30%

10.1 - 20%

10% and below

data not available

Extreme range: Botswana 51.82% — Guinea-Bissau 3.61%

Source: ILO Yearbook of Labour Statistics 1978, 1979

UNION OF SOVIET SOCIALIST REPUBLICS

MONGOLIA

CHINA

TURKEY
93

CYPRUS
SYRIA
84 **94** IRAQ
LEBANON
ISRAEL
33 JORDAN
39

IRAN
64

AFGHANISTAN

KUWAIT
57
BAHRAIN **51**
QATAR
U.A.E.

SAUDI
ARABIA

N
YEMEN S.
YEMEN
88

OMAN

EGYPT
0

JORDAN

ETHIOPIA

SOMALIA

UGANDA
71

KENYA

TANZANIA
87

COMOROS

MADAGASCAR

MOZAMBIQUE

MALAWI
ZAMBIA
ZIMBABWE
5

SWAZILAND **32**

LESOTHO

MAURITIUS **19**

PAKISTAN
89

NEPAL
29 BHUTAN

B-
DESH

INDIA
63

BURMA

SRI LANKA
70

N
KOREA
S. **86**

JAPAN
73

RYUKYU IS.
55

TAIWAN

HONG KONG
23

LAOS
THAILAND
85

VIETNAM

KAMPU-
CHEA
90

PHILIPPINES
59

BRUNEI

MALAYSIA
SINGAPORE
26

INDONESIA
67

PAPUA
NEW GUINEA

AUSTRALIA
12

NEW ZEALAND
34

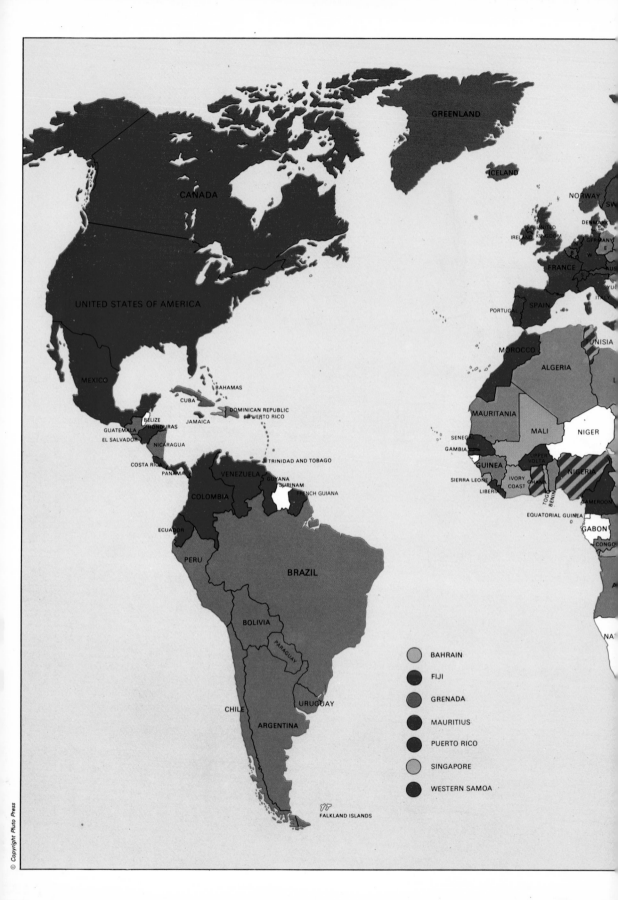

GREENLAND

ICELAND

CANADA

NORWAY

SW

DENMARK

IRELAND

UNITED
KINGDOM

GERMANY

E

B

O

W

FRANCE

AUS

UNITED STATES OF AMERICA

YU

PORTUGAL

SPAIN

ITALY

MEXICO

BAHAMAS

TUNISIA

MOROCCO

CUBA

DOMINICAN REPUBLIC

ALGERIA

L

JAMAICA

PUERTO RICO

BELIZE

HONDURAS

MAURITANIA

MALI

NIGER

GUATEMALA

EL SALVADOR

NICARAGUA

SENEGAL

COSTA RICA

GAMBIA

PANAMA

TRINIDAD AND TOBAGO

GUINEA

UPPER
VOLTA

NIGERIA

VENEZUELA

GUYANA

SIERRA LEONE

IVORY
COAST

GHANA

COLOMBIA

SURINAM

LIBERIA

TOGO

BENIN

CAMEROON

FRENCH GUIANA

EQUATORIAL GUINEA

GABON

ECUADOR

CONGO

PERU

BRAZIL

BOLIVIA

PARAGUAY

NA

CHILE

URUGUAY

ARGENTINA

○ BAHRAIN

● FIJI

● GRENADA

● MAURITIUS

● PUERTO RICO

○ SINGAPORE

● WESTERN SAMOA

FALKLAND ISLANDS

42. The Force of Labour

UNION OF SOVIET SOCIALIST REPUBLICS

MONGOLIA

TURKEY

RUS
BANON
SYRIA
ISRAEL
JORDAN
IRAQ
KUWAIT
IRAN
AFGHANISTAN
QATAR
U A E
OMAN
SAUDI ARABIA

YPT

DAN

N
YEMEN
S YEMEN

ETHIOPIA

SOMALIA

UGANDA
KENYA

TANZANIA

MALAWI

MBABWE

MOZAMBIQUE

MADAGASCAR

PAKISTAN

INDIA

NEPAL
BHUTAN
B
DESH
BURMA

SRI LANKA

CHINA

N
KOREA
S

JAPAN

TAIWAN

HONG KONG

LAOS

THAILAND
VIETNAM
KAM

MALAYSIA
SINGAPORE
W

PHILIPPINES

INDONESIA

PAPUA NEW
GUINEA

AUSTRALIA

NEW ZEALAND

**Degree of trade union independence,
early 1978**

unions independent and comprise more
than half the labour force

unions independent and comprise
less than half the labour force

unions nominally independent but
totally controlled

unions nominally independent but
tightly controlled

unions nominally independent but
severely repressed

virtually no recognised trade unionism

data not available

Source: Leading international trade union officials

Shares of world income and
world population compared

Rich countries

20% world population
68% world income
= rich 'market economies'

9% world population
15% world income
= rich 'centrally-planned economies'

Poor countries

48% world population
12% world income
= poor 'market economies'

22% world population
5% world income
= Asian 'centrally-planned economies'

Incomes of the top 5% compared
with the bottom 20%
1960s and early 1970s

more than 30 times as much

21 — 30 times as much

11 — 20 times as much

6 — 10 times as much

1 — 5 times as much

less than the bottom 20%

data not available

Source: Shail Jain, Size Distribution of Income:
a compilation of Data, World Bank 1975

GREENLAND

ICELAND

NORWAY SWE

DENMARK

IRELAND UNITED
KINGDOM W E
GERMANY
CZE

FRANCE AUST

CANADA

YUG

ITALY

UNITED STATES OF AMERICA

SPAIN

PORTUGAL

TUNISIA
☠ 1958

MOROCCO
☠
1960

ALGERIA
☠
1962

MEXICO

BAHAMAS

MAURITANIA
☠ 1960
1971-74

MALI
☠ 1971-74

NIGER
☠
1971-74

CUBA

DOMINICAN REPUBLIC

CAPE VERDE

PUERTO RICO

JAMAICA

BELIZE

HONDURAS

☠ HAITI
1954
1975-76

SENEGAL
☠ 1971-75
1977

UPPER
VOLTA

GUATEMALA

GAMBIA ☠
1973

GUINEA-BISSAU

NIGERIA
☠ 1967-70
1971-74

EL SALVADOR

☠ NICARAGUA
1951 1972

BARBADOS

GUINEA

TRINIDAD AND TOBAGO

BENIN

COSTA RICA

PANAMA

VENEZUELA

SIERRA LEONE

LIBERIA

IVORY
COAST
☠ 1971-74
1977-78

CAMEROON

GUYANA
SURINAM

☠ 1971-74
1977
TOGO

GABON
CONGO

COLOMBIA
☠
1987

ECUADOR

A

BRAZIL

PERU
☠
1970

NAM

BOLIVIA

PARAGUAY

CHILE
☠
1960

URUGUAY

ARGENTINA

FIJI

HONG KONG

SINGAPORE

The Sahel drought
1973

MOROCCO

ALGERIA

LIBYA

EGYPT

MAURITANIA

MALI

NIGER

CHAD

SENEGAL ☠

☠

GAMBIA

☠ UPPER
VOLTA

SUDAN

GUINEA-BISSAU

GUINEA

SIERRA LEONE

IVORY
COAST

GHANA
TOGO
BENIN

NIGERIA

CAR

LIBERIA

UNION OF SOVIET SOCIALIST REPUBLICS

MONGOLIA

CHINA

JAPAN

KOREA
N **1950-57**
1959
S

TURKEY
1962
SYRIA
LEBANON
ISRAEL
IRAQ
1954
IRAN
AFGHANISTAN
1971-72
PAKISTAN
1950-56
1960
1971-73
NEPAL
B
INDIA
1950-55
1965-67
1972
B-
DESH
1970-75
BURMA
LAOS
TAIWAN
1959
HONG KONG

QATAR
U.A.E.
OMAN
SAUDI ARABIA

DAN
N
YEMEN
S YEMEN
DJIBOUTI
ETHIOPIA
1973-79

SRI LANKA
THAILAND
VIETNAM
1954
1961
1964
1968
1975
KAM
1970
1975-76
1978-9

PHILIPPINES
1972

SOMALIA
1974-75
UGANDA
KENYA
1976

TANZANIA

MALAWI

MADAGASCAR
MOZAMBIQUE

1979

ABWE

1971-74

1974

BRUNEI
W
MALAYSIA

INDONESIA

1977

1975-79

PAPUA
NEW GUINEA

AUSTRALIA

Food and famines

**Calories available per head
as a proportion of estimated requirement
1972-74**

below requirement:

over 20% below

10.1 — 20% below

0.1 — 10% below

above requirement:

0.1 — 10% above

10.1 — 20% above

20.1 — 30% above

over 30% above

data not available

Extreme range: Upper Volta 27% below requirement—
Czechoslovakia, Ireland, Portugal 41% above requirement

Countries with major famines 1950-79

NEW ZEALAND

Source: FAO Fourth World Food Survey, 1977 Science, 9 May 1975, and the press

GREENLAND

NORWA
68 75

72 78

ICELAND
73 79   68 74   72 78   72

UNITED KINGDOM
SW
DENMARK

CANADA
69 76

IRELAND
69 74   68 74   W E
GERMANY   CZ
AUS
S
70 77
FRANCE   ITALY

UNITED STATES OF AMERICA
69 77   65 72   70 75   69
PORTUGAL   SPAIN

53 56
TUNISIA

51 4

MOROCCO
51 55

52 55   51 5

CUBA   BAHAMAS
69 72
ALGERIA

MEXICO
63 67   DOMINICAN REPUBLIC
57 59

HAITI   JAMAICA
52 55   63 67
GUATEMALA
48 50   51 55   PUERTO RICO   69 76
EL SALVADOR   NICARAGUA   BARBADOS   MAURITANIA   37 40 MALI
57 60   39 42   37 40   37 40
COSTA RICA   59 63   CAPE   NIGER
66 70   PANAMA   VENEZUELA   GUYANA   VERDE   SENEGAL   37 37
65 67   63 67   59 63   39 42
COLOMBIA   SURINAM   GAMBIA   32 31
FR GUYANA   GUINEA-BISSAU   U. VOLTA   BENIN
ECUADOR   SIERRA LEONE   39   42   GUINEA   42 45   39 43 CAM
54 58   42 45   LIBERIA   IVORY   TOGO
46 44   COAST   GABON
53 55   GHANA 42 45   CONGO
PERU   32 39
BRAZIL
58 61   39   43
ALBANIA
65 67
BOLIVIA   42 45
AUSTRIA   46 48
68 75
PAR   25 45
HAITI   60 64
49 51   42 45   AN
HONG KONG
67 75   NAMIBIA
CHILE   URUGUAY
HUNGARY   66 72   39
67 72   60 66
LUXEMBOURG   ARGENTINA
67 74   65 71
SWITZERLAND
70 76
TRINIDAD AND TOBAGO
64 68
YUGOSLAVIA
65 70

Infant mortality		Life expectancy	
Deaths in first year of life Europe and N. America 1976-77 others 1970-75		52 55	
	below 20	Hospital beds per 100,000 population where data available	
	20 - 50	over 600	
	51-100	401 — 600	
	101-150	201 — 400	
	151-200	200 and below	
	over 200		
	data not available		

Source: UN Statistical Yearbook 1978, UN Demographic Yearbook 1977

© Copyright Pluto Press

UNION OF SOVIET SOCIALIST REPUBLICS

69 74

87 75

67 74

72

69 74

54 54

IRAQ

58 57

40 41

54 49

IRAN

AFGH

PAKISTAN

66 72

inset KUWAIT

U ARAB EMIRATES

SAUDI ARABIA

OMAN

44 46

44 46

39 43

SOMALIA

N YEM

S YEMEN

37 40

ETHIOPIA

49 52

47 51

KENYA

39 43

41 41

40 43

COMOROS

MALAWI

MOZAMBIQUE

BWE

42 45

38 38

MADAGASCAR

S

42 45

41 44

50 53

48

64 74

60 62

MONGOLIA

60 63

CHINA

42 45

42 45

NEPAL

B

42 41

46 47

49 52

BURMA

LA

59 63

KOREA

SA

63 67

72 77

JAPAN

TAIWAN

39 42

44 43

VIETNAM

PHILIPPINES

57 60

43 46

KAM

54 59

THAILAND

BANGLADESH

65 67

65 70

SRI LANKA

SINGAPORE

MALAYSIA

48 48

INDONESIA

48 48

PAPUA
NEW GUINEA

68 74

AUSTRALIA

inset

70 73

CYPRUS

54 59

SYRIA

LEBANON

61 65

71 75

ISRAEL

51 54

IRAQ

JORDAN

53 52

SAUDI ARABIA

44 47

69 75

NEW ZEALAND

EGYPT

DAN

50

CANADA

ICELAND

NORWAY

SWEDEN

IRELAND

UNITED KINGDOM

DENMARK

N
B
L

EAST
GERMANY

POLAND

CZECH

FRANCE

SWITZ AUSTRIA

HUNGA

WEST
GERMANY

PORTUGAL

SPAIN

ITALY

YUGO

ALB

GREECE

Primary & Secondary 87%

UNITED STATES OF AMERICA

MEXICO

BAHAMAS

CUBA

JAMAICA

HAITI

DOMINICAN REPUBLIC

PUERTO RICO

GUATEMALA

EL SALVADOR

HONDURAS

NICARAGUA

COSTA RICA

PANAMA

BARBADOS

TRIN

VENEZUELA

GUYANA

SURINAM

COLOMBIA

ECUADOR

PERU

BRAZIL

MOROCCO

ALGERIA

TUNISIA

LIB

MAURITANIA

MALI

NIGER

GAMBIA

SENEGAL

GUINEA

GUINEA-BISSAU

VOLTA

IVORY
COAST

GHANA

TOGO

BENIN

NIGERIA

CAMERO

GABON

CONG

SIERRA LEONE

LIBERIA

EQUATORIAL GUINEA

N

ALBANIA

AUSTRIA

BELGIUM

BULGARIA

NETHERLANDS

BURUNDI

ROMANIA

CZECHOSLOVAKIA

RWANDA

EAST GERMANY

SINGAPORE

LUXEMBOURG

SWITZERLAND

MALTA

UPPER VOLTA

MAURITIUS

ZIMBABWE

BOLIVIA

PARAGUAY

ARGENTINA

URUGUAY

CHILE

FALKLAND ISLANDS

Literacy

Adult illiterates as a proportion of
the population 15 years old and over

- over 80%
- 61 — 80%
- 41 — 60%
- 21 — 40%
- 20% and below
- data not available

Extreme range: Niger 98.6% — USSR 0.3%

Copyright Pluto Press

Education

**Primary school enrolment
as proportion of population 6—11 years old**

| 50% and below | 50.1 — 90% | over 90% |

Extreme range: Gabon 202% — Bhutan 12%

**Secondary school enrolment
as proportion of population 12—18 years old**

| 25% and below | 25.2—50% | over 50% |

Extreme range: Finland 97% — Bhutan 1%

**Enrolment in tertiary level education
as proportion of population 20—24 years old**

| 5% and below | 5.1—20% | over 20% |

Extreme range: USA 57.64% — for example,
Equatorial Guinea, Gambia, Mauritania,
Bhutan, with none

Source: UNESCO Statistical Yearbook 1977

GREENLAND

NETHERLANDS
BELGIUM
ICELAND
NORWAY
DENM
IRELAND
UNITED
KINGDOM
GERMANY
LUXEMBOURG
FRANCE
ITALY
PORTUGAL
SPAIN
SWITZERLAND
TUNISIA

CANADA

UNITED STATES OF AMERICA

MEXICO
BAHAMAS
CUBA
JAMAICA
DOMINICAN REPUBLIC
HAITI
BELIZE
PUERTO RICO
GUATEMALA
HONDURAS
EL SALVADOR
NICARAGUA
BARBADOS
COSTA RICA
TRINIDAD AND TOBAGO
PANAMA
VENEZUELA
GUYANA
SURINAM
COLOMBIA

MOROCCO
ALGERIA
MAURITANIA
MALI
NIGER
GAMBIA
SENEGAL
GUINEA-BISSAU
UPPER
VOLTA
BENIN
GUINEA
SIERRA LEONE
IVORY
COAST
GHANA
NIGERIA
LIBERIA
TOGO
EQUATORIAL GUINEA
CAMEROON
GABON
CONGO

ECUADOR
PERU
BRAZIL

BOLIVIA

NAM

CHILE
PARAGUAY
URUGUAY
ARGENTINA

FIJI

HONG KONG

MAURITIUS

WESTERN SAMOA

**Newsprint consumption
per head in 1977**

	above 15 kilogrammes
	10.1—15 kilogrammes
	5.1—10 kilogrammes
	1.1—5 kilogrammes
	1 kilogramme and below
	data not available

Source UN Statistical Yearbook 1978

UNION OF SOVIET SOCIALIST REPUBLICS

MONGOLIA

N' KOREA

S. KOREA

JAPAN

CHINA

TURKEY

RUS

CYP

SYRIA

ISRAEL

JORDAN

IRAQ

KUWAIT

IRAN

AFGHANISTAN

PAKISTAN

SAUDI ARABIA

QATAR

UNITED ARAB EMIRATES

NEPAL

BHUTAN

BANGLADESH

BURMA

TAIWAN

HONG KONG

EGYPT

N YEMEN

S YEMEN

OMAN

INDIA

LAOS

THAILAND

VIETNAM

KAM

PHILIPPINES

SUDAN

ETHIOPIA

SOMALIA

SRI LANKA

BRUNEI

MALAYSIA

UGANDA

KENYA

SINGAPORE

TANZANIA

INDONESIA

PAPUA NEW GUINEA

MALAWI

MAURITIUS

MOZAMBIQUE

MADAGASCAR

ZIMBABWE

LESOTHO

AUSTRALIA

Telephones per 1000 population in 1976

Where data available

over 500

401 — 500

301 — 400

201 — 300

101 — 200

11 — 101

10 and below

AUSTRIA

BAHRAIN

FIJI

WESTERN SAMOA

NEW ZEALAND

Source UN Statistical Yearbook 1978

CANADA

ICELAND

NORWAY

UNITED KINGDOM
IRELAND
DENMARK
NETH.
BELG.
GERMANY
FRANCE
SWIT.

UNITED STATES OF AMERICA

PORTUGAL
SPAIN

TUNISIA

MOROCCO
ALGERIA

MEXICO

BAHAMAS

CUBA
HAITI
DOMINICAN REPUBLIC
JAMAICA
PUERTO RICO

MAURITANIA
MALI
NIGER

GUATEMALA
HONDURAS
EL SALVADOR
NICARAGUA
COSTA RICA
PANAMA

GRENADA
BARBADOS
TRINIDAD AND TOBAGO

SENEGAL
GAMBIA
GUINEA-BISSAU
SIERRA LEONE
LIBERIA

GUINEA
IVORY
COAST

UPPER
VOLTA

GHANA
TOGO
BENIN

NIGERIA

VENEZUELA
GUYANA
SURINAM

COLOMBIA

CAMEROON

EQUATORIAL GUINEA

GABON
CONGO

ECUADOR

PERU

BRAZIL

BOLIVIA

PARAGUAY

URUGUAY

CHILE

ARGENTINA

FALKLAND ISLANDS

MAURITIUS

Welfare receipts as a proportion of GDP
1974 or most recent year

2% and below	10.1 — 15%
2.1 — 5%	above 15%
5.1 — 10%	data not available

Extreme range: Singapore 0.44% — Sweden 20.74%

Source: ILO

CANADA

UNITED STATES OF AMERICA

MEXICO

BAHAMAS

CUBA

JAMAICA

HAITI   DOMINICAN REPUBLIC

PUERTO RICO

GUATEMALA   HONDURAS

EL SALVADOR

NICARAGUA

COSTA RICA

PANAMA

VENEZUELA

GUYANA

SURINAM

COLOMBIA

ECUADOR

PERU

BRAZIL

BOLIVIA

PARAGUAY

CHILE

URUGUAY

ARGENTINA

BARBADOS

TRINIDAD AND TOBAGO

NORWAY

SWEDEN

DENMARK

IRELAND

UNITED KINGDOM

NETHERLANDS

BELGIUM

EAST GERMANY

WEST GERMANY

POLA

CZECHOSLOVA

FRANCE

SWITZ

AUSTRIA

HU

YUGOSL

ITALY

PORTUGAL

SPAIN

AL

MOROCCO

TUNISIA

ALGERIA

LI

MAURITANIA

MALI

NIGER

SENEGAL

GAMBIA

GUINEA

UPPER VOLTA

BEN IN

NIGERIA

SIERRA LEONE

IVORY COAST

LIBERIA

GHANA

CAMEROON

EQUATORIAL GUINEA

GABON

CONGO

AN

NAM

Growth in urban population 1950-75

- over 400%
- 301 — 400%
- 201 — 300%
- 101 — 200%
- 51 — 100%
- 50% and below
- urban decline
- data not available

Extreme range: N. and S. Yemen
688% growth — East Germany 1.5% decline

decline in rural population

Source: UN, World Population Trends and Policies, 1977.
Monitoring Report Vol. 1, 1979

UNION OF SOVIET SOCIALIST REPUBLICS

MONGOLIA

KOREA
N
S

JAPAN

TURKEY

CYPRUS
SYRIA
LEB
ISRAEL
IRAQ
JORDAN
PT
DAN

IRAN

AFGHANISTAN

CHINA

KUWAIT
QATAR
U A E
OMAN

SAUDI ARABIA

YEMEN
S YEMEN

PAKISTAN

NEPAL
BH
H
DESH

INDIA

BURMA

LAOS

THAILAND

TAIWAN

HONG KONG

KAM
VIETNAM

PHILIPPINES

SRI LANKA

ETHIOPIA

SOMALIA

UGAN
DA
KENYA

B

TANZANIA

MALAWI

BWE
MOZAMBIQUE

MADAGASCAR

S

MALAYSIA

W

INDONESIA

PAPUA
NEW
GUINEA

AUSTRALIA

NEW ZEALAND

GREENLAND

ICELAND

NORWAY

CANADA

DENMARK

IRELAND UNITED KINGDOM

N W E GERMANY S

UNITED STATES OF AMERICA

FRANCE

ITALY

PORTUGAL SPAIN

Rabat

Casablanca

MOROCCO

TUNISIA

MEXICO

BAHAMAS

ALGERIA

Mexico City

CUBA

DOMINICAN REPUBLIC

JAMAICA HAITI

PUERTO RICO

MAURITANIA

MALI

NIGER

Guatemala City

Santo Domingo

GUATEMALA HONDURAS

Dakar

EL SALVADOR Tegucigalpa

SENEGAL

NICARAGUA

Cartagena Maracaibo

BARBADOS

GAMBIA

Ouagadougou

COSTA RICA

Caracas

Barquisimeto

TRINIDAD AND TOBAGO

GUINEA

UPPER VOLTA

BENIN

NIGERIA

Panama City

Ciudad Guayana

SIERRA LEONE

IVORY

Ibadan

PANAMA

VENEZUELA

GUYANA

COAST

Accra

CAM

Buenaventura

Bogotá

SURINAM

Monrovia

Abidjan

Douala

COLOMBIA

LIBERIA

GHANA

Ya

Cali

Lome

ECUADOR

TOGO

GABON

Guayaquil

EQUATORIAL

CONG

GUINEA

PERU

Recife

BRAZIL

Chimbote

Lima

Brasilia

Arequipa

BOLIVIA

Belo Horizonte

CHILE

PARAGUAY

Rio de Janeiro

ARGENTINA

Porto Alegre

URUGUAY

Santiago

Buenos Aires

UNION OF SOVIET SOCIALIST REPUBLICS

MONGOLIA

CHINA

JAPAN

N KOREA
Seoul
Pusan
S KOREA

stanbul
Ankara
TURKEY
YPRUS SYRIA
LEBANON
ISRAEL Amman Baghdad
JORDAN
IRAQ
IRAN
KUWAIT
QATAR
UAE OMAN
SAUDI ARABIA
Port Sudan
N YEMEN S YEMEN
YPT
UDAN

AFGHANISTAN
Kabul
PAKISTAN
Karachi
Delhi
Ahmadabad
Agra
NEPAL Katmandu
BHU
Baroda
INDIA
Calcutta
Dacca
BANGLADESH
Bombay
BURMA
LAOS
Bangalore
Madras
THAILAND
SRI LANKA
Colombo

TAIWAN
HONG KONG

VIETNAM
Phnom Penh
Bangkok
KAM

Manila
PHILIPPINES

ETHIOPIA
Addis Ababa
SOMALIA
Mogadishu
UGAN DA
KENYA
Nairobi
B
Mombasa
TANZANIA
Dar-es-Salaam
AMBIA Blantyre MALAWI
BABWE
MOZAMBIQUE
MADAGASCAR
Tananarive
S

Kuala Lumpur
MALAYSIA
SING APORE

INDONESIA

PAPUA NEW GUINEA

AUSTRALIA

Housing and urban slums

Proportion of population without a safe water supply in 1976

- 20% and below
- 21 - 40%
- 41 - 60%
- 61 - 80%
- over 80%
- data not available

Extreme range: Bahrain, Denmark, Iceland, Israel, Sweden and UK 1% – Gabon 99%

Proportion of city populations in slum and squatter settlements late 1960s and early 1970s

- 20% and below
- 21 - 40%
- 41 - 60%
- 61 - 80%
- over 80%

Source: R.L. Sivard, World Military and Social Expenditures 1979.
UN, World Housing Survey 1974

NEW ZEALAND

CANADA

UNITED STATES OF AMERICA

MEXICO

BAHAMAS

CUBA

HAITI DOMINICAN REPUBLIC
JAMAICA PUERTO RICO

GUATEMALA HONDURAS
EL SALVADOR

NICARAGUA

COSTA RICA

PANAMA

BARBADOS
TRINIDAD AND TOBAGO

GUYANA

VENEZUELA SURINAM

COLOMBIA

ECUADOR

PERU

BRAZIL

BOLIVIA

PARAGUAY

CHILE

URUGUAY

ARGENTINA

ICELAND

NETHERLANDS

LUXEMBOURG

NORWAY

SWEDEN

IRELAND

UNITED
KINGDOM

DENMARK

BELGIUM

GERMANY
EAST
WEST

POLAND

CZECHOSLOVAKIA

AUSTRIA

HUNGARY

FRANCE

SWITZ

PORTUGAL

SPAIN

YUGOSLAVIA

ITALY

ALBANIA

TUNISIA

MOROCCO

ALGERIA

MAURITANIA

MALI

NIGER

SENEGAL

GAMBIA

GUINEA

UPPER
VOLTA

SIERRA LEONE

BENIN

NIGERIA

LIBERIA

IVORY
COAST

GHANA

EQUATORIAL
GUINEA

CAMEROON

GABON

CONGO

○ BAHRAIN

○ FIJI

● MALTA

● MAURITIUS

○ MONACO

● NETHERLANDS ANTILLES

● ST.KITTS-NEVIS-ANGUILLA

● SINGAPORE

○ SOLOMON ISLANDS

Murder

**Murders recorded for every 100,000 population
Annual average 1973-76 or nearest equivalent**

- 2 and below
- 2.1 - 5
- 5.1 - 10
- 10.1 - 15
- above 15
- data not available

Extreme range: Bahrain .2 - Nigeria 40.7

Source: Interpol, International Crime Statistics
US Dept. of Commerce, Bureau of the Census,
Statistical Abstract of the United States.

UNION OF SOVIET SOCIALIST REPUBLICS

MONGOLIA

CHINA

N KOREA

S KOREA

JAPAN

TAIWAN

SYRIA

IRAQ

IRAN

AFGHANISTAN

PAKISTAN

NEPAL

BHU

INDIA

BANGLADESH

BURMA

LAOS

THAILAND

KAMPU CHEA

S VIETNAM

HONG KONG

PHILIPPINES

KUWAIT

QATAR

U.A.E

OMAN

SAUDI ARABIA

N Y

S YEMEN

ETHIOPIA

SOMALIA

SRI LANKA

MALAYSIA

SINGAPORE

INDONESIA

PAPUA NEW GUINEA

KENYA

TANZANIA

MALAWI

BIA

ABWE

MOZAMBIQUE

MADAGASCAR

AUSTRALIA

inset

TURKEY

CYPRUS

SYRIA

LEBANON

IRAQ

ISRAEL

JORDAN

SAUDI ARABIA

Crime

Crimes recorded (other than traffic offences)
for every 100,000 population

Annual average 1973-76 or nearest equivalent
Where data available

| 1000 and under | 1001 -3000 | 3001 -5000 | above 5000 |

Extreme range: Philippines 81 — Lebanon 34,791

NEW ZEALAND

Unemployment throughout the world is
enormous and growing. This is admitted
everywhere, but official statistics tend to
disguise rather than reveal the extent. For this
reason it has been impossible to produce a
useful map on the problem. Instead this
diagram shows a projected growth in world
population and its division into employed
labour force and inactive population, 1750-2150

year

2150

2100

2050

2000

**Projected growth in world population
and division into
employed labour force and inactive population**

employed labour force

inactive population including unemployed

world population

Source: ILO

people

11000 million   10000 million   9000 million   8000 million   7000 million   6000 million   5000 million

South Asia
East Asia
Africa
Latin America

Europe
USSR
North America
Oceania

year

2150

2100

2050

2000

1970 — 1970

1900 — 1900

1850 — 1850

1800 — 1800

1750 — 1750

lion · 3000 million · 2000 million · 1000 million · 0 · 0 · 1000 million · 2000 million

people

CANADA

GREENLAND

Thule

Kap Tobin

ICELAND

Helena

Moosonee

Salt Lake City

Richmond

Rocky Flats

New York

UNITED STATES OF AMERICA

IRELAND

UNITED
KINGDOM

London

FR

PORTUGAL

SPAIN

Madrid

MEXICO

CUBA

BAHAMAS

JAMAICA

DOMINICAN REPUBLIC

BELIZE
HONDURAS

HAITI

GUATEMALA
EL SALVADOR

NICARAGUA

BARBADOS

TRINIDAD AND TOBAGO

COSTA RICA

Balboa

PANAMA

VENEZUELA

GUYANA

SURINAM

COLOMBIA

ECUADOR

Guayaquil

PERU

Lima

BRAZIL

BOLIVIA

PARAGUAY

CHILE

URUGUAY

ARGENTINA

Miami

MOROCCO

ALGERIA

TUNISIA

MAURITANIA

MALI

NIGER

SENEGAL
GAMBIA

GUINEA-BISSAU

GUINEA

UPPER
VOLTA

NIGERIA

SIERRA LEONE

IVORY
COAST

GHANA

BENIN

TOGO

LIBERIA

CAMEROON

EQUATORIAL GUINEA

GABON

CONGO

NA

Lead pollution
One example in the Western Hemisphere

10 femtocuries per cubic metre

FALKLAND
ISLANDS

Principal areas of damage to the sea

pollution

Source: US Energy Research and Development
Association, Health and Safety Laboratory

Source: Earthscan

**Sulphuric acid/sulphur dioxide pollution
Two examples: Europe and Japan**

100 micrograms per cubic metre

*Source: World Health Organization, Global
Environmental Monitoring System 1976*

UNION OF SOVIET SOCIALIST REPUBLICS

Pollution in the Mediterranean

★ focal points

▉ tar (10 milligrams per square metre)

▨ sewage and fertilizer
(100,000 tons per year)

Source: UN Evironmental Program 1977

The Sands of Negligence

'More than one third of the earth's land is arid. Much of it has become desert since the dawn of civilization, and many vulnerable areas are even now being turned into desert. This process has intensified in recent decades, and threatens the future of 628 million people or that 14 per cent of the world's population who live in the drylands; of this number, between 50 and 78 million people are affected directly by decreases in productivity associated with current desertification processes.
In the past half century, on the southern edge of the Sahara alone, as much as 650,000 sq. km of once productive land has become desert.'

Report of UN Conference on Desertification,1977

Source: UN World Map of Desertification 1977

Bioclimatic zones
- hyper-arid
- arid
- semi-arid
- sub-humid
- humid

Areas of risk
- very high
- moderate
- highly vulnerable land
- high human/mechanical pressure
- high animal pressure

UNION OF SOVIET SOCIALIST REPUBLICS

MONGOLIA

N KOREA
S KOREA
JAPAN

CHINA

TAIWAN

SYRIA
IRAQ
IRAN
AFGHANISTAN
KUWAIT
QATAR
U.A.E
SAUDI
ARABIA
OMAN
S. YEMEN
N YEMEN
PAKISTAN
NEPAL
BHUTAN
BAN
INDIA
BURMA

LAOS
THAILAND
KAMP
VIETNAM

PHILIPPINES

ETHIOPIA
SOMALIA
UGANDA
KENYA

SRI LANKA

MALAYSIA

INDONESIA

PAPUA
NEW
GUINEA

TANZANIA
MALAWI
MOZAMBIQUE
MADAGASCAR

AUSTRALIA

Murdered Land

War pollution in
Vietnam,
Kampuchea and
Laos 1965-70

NORTH VIETNAM
7.1%

Hue
10.3%

LAOS
10.2%

Military Region 1
100.1%

4.7% Pleiku

23.2%
SOUTH
VIETNAM

KAMPUCHEA

R. Mekong

4.4%

Phnom Penh

123.7% Military Region 2

30%
Saigon
Military Region 3

4%

South China Sea

11.6%
Military Region 4

proportion of surface area
of each military region

bombarded with flying
'shrapnel' or metal shards

sprayed with herbicides

NEW ZEALAND

Changes in industrial growth

Average annual increase/decrease in industrial growth rate between 1960-70 and 1970-78

Increase in growth rate:

over 50%

25 — 50%

up to 25%

Decrease in growth rate:

up to 25%

25 — 50%

over 50%

data not available

manufacturing only

Extreme range: Morocco 86.9% increase — Mozambique, Chile, Venezuela: absolute decline in 1970-78

Source: UN Monthly Bulletin of Statistics, November 1979
UN Statistical Yearbook, 1978

UNION OF SOVIET SOCIALIST REPUBLICS

MONGOLIA

CHINA

N KOREA
S

JAPAN

TURKEY

CYPRUS
LEBANON
ISRAEL
SYRIA
IRAQ
IRAN
AFGHANISTAN

KUWAIT
QATAR
SAUDI ARABIA
U.A.E.
OMAN
N YEMEN
S YEMEN

PAKISTAN

NEPAL
BHUTAN
B-DESH
INDIA
BURMA
LAOS
TAIWAN

EGYPT

SUDAN

ETHIOPIA
SOMALIA

KENYA

UGANDA

TANZANIA

THAILAND
KAM
VIETNAM

PHILIPPINES

SRI LANKA

MALAYSIA

INDONESIA

PAPUA
NEW GUINEA

MALAWI

MOZAMBIQUE

MADAGASCAR

ZIMBABWE

AUSTRALIA

NEW ZEALAND

GREENLAND

ICELAND

FAROE ISLANDS

NORWAY

SWEDEN

DENMARK

IRELAND
UNITED
KINGDOM

N
B
W
GERMANY
E
CZ

FRANCE

S
AUS

ITALY

CANADA

PORTUGAL
SPAIN

UNITED STATES OF AMERICA

MOROCCO

TUNISIA

ALGERIA

L

MEXICO

BAHAMAS

CUBA

HAITI
DOMINICAN REPUBLIC
PUERTO RICO

BELIZE
JAMAICA
HONDURAS

GUATEMALA

EL SALVADOR

NICARAGUA

COSTA RICA
PANAMA

CAPE VERDE

MAURITANIA

MALI

NIGER

SENEGAL
GAMBIA
GUINEA-BISSAU

UPPER
VOLTA

NIGERIA

BARBADOS

TRINIDAD AND TOBAGO

VENEZUELA

GUYANA
SURINAM

GUINEA

SIERRA LEONE

IVORY
COAST

GHANA

BENIN
TOGO

LIBERIA

COLOMBIA

EQUATORIAL GUINEA

CAMEROON

ECUADOR

GABON

CONGO

PERU

BRAZIL

AN

BOLIVIA

PARAGUAY

NAM

CHILE

URUGUAY

ARGENTINA

⚡ FALKLAND ISLANDS

○ BAHRAIN

● MAURITIUS

○ SINGAPORE

UNION OF SOVIET SOCIALIST REPUBLICS

MONGOLIA

TURKEY

US LEB
SYRIA
ISRAEL
IRAQ
KUWAIT
IRAN
AFGHANISTAN
CHINA
N
KOREA
S
JAPAN
PAKISTAN
NEPAL
SAUDI
ARABIA
QATAR
UAE
OMAN
BH
B.
DESH
INDIA
BURMA
LAOS
HONG
KONG
VIETNAM
MARIANAS
N
YEMEN
S YEMEN
DJIBOUTI
THAILAND
KAM
PHILIPPINES
PT
DAN
ETHIOPIA
SOMALIA
SRI LANKA
MALDIVES
KIRIBATI (GILBERT ISLANDS)
UGANDA
KENYA
BRUNEI
N
MALAYSIA
SINGAPORE
TANZANIA
MALAWI
COMOROS
INDONESIA
PAPUA
NEW GUINEA
ABWE
MADAGASCAR
S

AUSTRALIA

Annual inflation rates, 1974

- over 50%
- 25.1 — 50%
- 20.1 — 25%
- 15.1 — 20%
- 10.1 — 15%
- 5.1 — 10%
- below 5%
- data not available

Extreme range: Chile 585.9%
— Niger 3.6%

Source: IMF Industrial Financial Statistics,
April 1977

NEW
ZEALAND

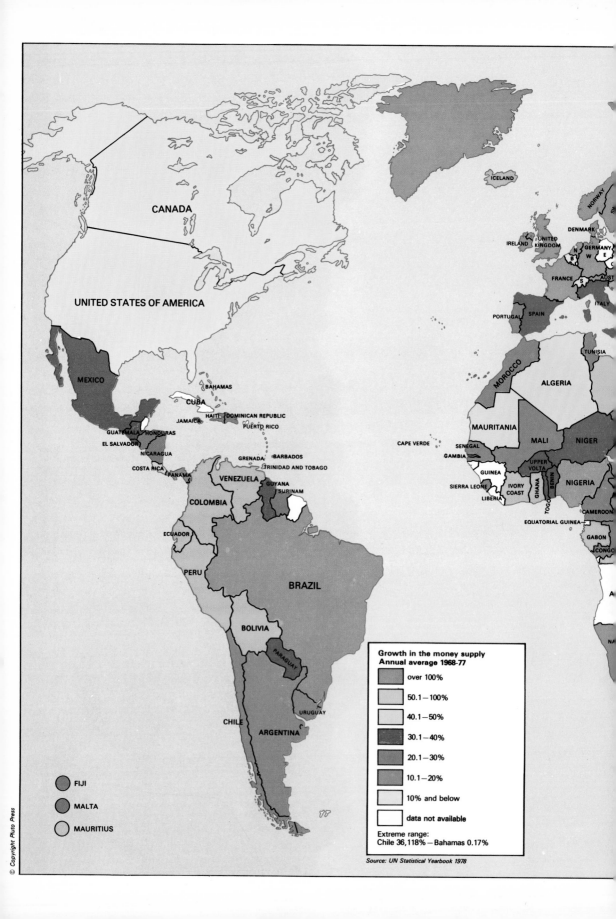

CANADA

UNITED STATES OF AMERICA

MEXICO

BAHAMAS

CUBA

HAITI DOMINICAN REPUBLIC

JAMAICA PUERTO RICO

GUATEMALA HONDURAS

EL SALVADOR

NICARAGUA

COSTA RICA

PANAMA

GRENADA BARBADOS

TRINIDAD AND TOBAGO

VENEZUELA

GUYANA

SURINAM

COLOMBIA

ECUADOR

PERU

BRAZIL

BOLIVIA

PARAGUAY

URUGUAY

CHILE

ARGENTINA

ICELAND

NORWAY

DENMARK

IRELAND UNITED KINGDOM

GERMANY

N

B

W

E

S

FRANCE

AUST

ITALY

PORTUGAL SPAIN

TUNISIA

MOROCCO

ALGERIA

MAURITANIA

MALI

NIGER

CAPE VERDE

SENEGAL

GAMBIA

UPPER VOLTA

GUINEA

SIERRA LEONE

IVORY COAST

GHANA

TOGO

BENIN

NIGERIA

LIBERIA

CAMEROON

EQUATORIAL GUINEA

GABON

CONGO

A

NA

FIJI

MALTA

MAURITIUS

**Growth in the money supply
Annual average 1968-77**

over 100%

50.1 – 100%

40.1 – 50%

30.1 – 40%

20.1 – 30%

10.1 – 20%

10% and below

data not available

Extreme range:
Chile 36,118% – Bahamas 0.17%

Source: UN Statistical Yearbook 1978

UNION OF SOVIET SOCIALIST REPUBLICS

MONGOLIA

CHINA

N. KOREA JAPAN
S.

TURKEY

PRUS.
LEBANON
SYRIA
ISRAEL
JORDAN
IRAQ
IRAN
AFGHANISTAN
KUWAIT
PAKISTAN
BAHRAIN
QATAR
U.A.E.
OMAN
SAUDI ARABIA
NEPAL
BHUTAN
B-
DESH
BURMA
INDIA
THAILAND
VIETNAM
LAOS
KAM
TAIWAN
HONG KONG
PHILIPPINES

YPT
N
YEMEN
S
YEMEN
JDAN
ETHIOPIA
SOMALIA
SRI LANKA
UGANDA
KENYA
W
MALAYSIA
SINGAPORE
TANZANIA
INDONESIA
PAPUA
NEW GUINEA
ABWE
MADAGASCAR
MOZAMBIQUE
S

AUSTRALIA

**Decline in purchasing power
of national currencies 1950-75**

above 90%   51—60%

81—90%   50% and below

71—80%   data not available

61—70%

*Source: Pick's Currency Yearbook
1976-77*

Destruction of paper money

NEW
ZEALAND

CANADA

UNITED STATES OF AMERICA

ICELAND

NORWAY
SWED
DENMARK
IRELAND
UNITED
KINGDOM
N
B
W
E
GERMANY
CZE
FRANCE
AUST
S
YU
ITALY

*Other N. Atlantic countries
including transnationals 318.4%*
International institutions 323%

PORTUGAL   SPAIN

TUNISIA

MOROCCO

ALGERIA   L

*Other developing countries
(OPEC) 267%*

MEXICO

BAHAMAS

CUBA
JAMAICA
HAITI
DOMINICAN REPUBLIC
PUERTO RICO
GUATEMALA
EL SALVADOR
HONDURAS
NICARAGUA
COSTA RICA
PANAMA

MAURITANIA

MALI

NIGER

SENEGAL
GAMBIA
GUINEA-BISSAU
GUINEA
UPPER
VOLTA

BARBADOS
TRINIDAD AND TOBAGO

VENEZUELA
GUYANA
SURINAM
COLOMBIA

ECUADOR

PERU

*Other developing countries
(non-OPEC) 375%*

BRAZIL

BOLIVIA

CHILE

PARAGUAY

URUGUAY

ARGENTINA

Euro-currencies

Growth/decline in publicly-announced
Euro-currency bank credits between 1975 and 1979

Growth

more than 1000%

501 — 1000%

251 — 500%

250% and below

Decline

1979 less than 1975

data not available

Extreme range: Venezuela 19,137 % increase
— Japan, Iran 100% decrease

*Source: Morgan Guaranty Trust, World Financial
Markets, May 1978 and January 1980*

CANADA
15%

UNITED STATES OF AMERICA
15.25%

MEXICO
19%

BAHAMAS

CUBA
JAMAICA HAITI DOMINICAN REPUBLIC
HONDURAS   PUERTO RICO
GUATEMALA
EL SALVADOR
NICARAGUA
COSTA RICA
PANAMA

IRELAN
15.5%

BARBADOS
TRINIDAD AND TOBAGO
VENEZUELA
13%
GUYANA
SURINAM
COLOMBIA

ECUADOR

PERU

BRAZIL
61.82%

BOLIVIA

CHILE

PARAGUAY

URUGUAY

ARGENTINA

FALKLAND ISLANDS

*Source: Morgan Guaranty Trust, World Financial
Markets, November 1978 and January 1980*

UNION OF SOVIET SOCIALIST REPUBLICS

Other 'centrally-planned economies'
including COMECON institutions 242.7%
(increase mainly due to China's entry as a borrower in 1979)

MONGOLIA

CHINA

N KOREA

S KOREA

JAPAN

TURKEY

PRUS SYRIA
EBANON
ISRAEL IRAQ IRAN
J KUWAIT
QATAR
U A E OMAN
SAUDI ARABIA

AFGHANISTAN

PAKISTAN

NEPAL

B DESH

BURMA

TAIWAN

HONG KONG

INDIA

LAOS

THAILAND

VIETNAM

KAM

PHILIPPINES

PT

DAN

N YEMEN
S YEMEN
ETHIOPIA

MALAYSIA

INDONESIA

PAPUA
NEW GUINEA

AUSTRALIA

Inset map (Europe / Middle East / Asia)

NORWAY
11%

SWEDEN
13.75%

7.85% FINLAND

DENMARK
13.75%

NETHER-
LANDS
15%

GERMANY
WEST

EAST

POLAND

UNION OF
SOVIET SOCIALIST
REPUBLICS

N KOREA
S
18.5%

6.31% JAPAN

BELG
15.25%

9.75%

CZECHOSLOVAKIA

CHINA

NCE
65%

5%
SWITZ

AUSTRIA

HUNGARY

TAIWAN
14.5% HONG KONG

19.5%
ITALY

ROMANIA

YUGOSLAVIA

BULGARIA

KAM

THAILAND
S
9.5%
SINGAPORE

MALAYSIA

VIETNAM

PHILIPPINES
16%

INDONESIA

PAPUA
NEW
GUINEA

ZAIRE

TANZANIA

ANGOLA

ZAMBIA MALAWI

AMIBIA

ZIM

BOTS
9.5%

MOZAM-
BIQUE

MADAGASCAR

SOUTH
AFRICA

AUSTRALIA
10.75%

The Rising Cost of Money

Growth/decline in bank lending rates
to prime borrowers between 1975 and 1979

Growth	Decline
over 100%	0 — 25%
75.1 — 100%	over 25%
50.1 — 75%	data not available
25.1 — 50%	
0 — 25%	

*Figures on countries show
best lending rates of banks,
December 1979*

Hong Kong

Singapore

NEW ZEALAND
12%

NEW ZEALAND

CANADA

11.87

1.09

1.7

0.16

0.1

UNITED STATES OF AMERICA

0.06

0.32

0.16

0.23

MEXICO

BAHAMAS

CUBA

JAMAICA

HAITI DOMINICAN REPUBLIC
        PUERTO RICO

GUATEMALA HONDURAS
EL SALVADOR
        NICARAGUA

COSTA RICA
        PANAMA

0.05

GRENADA
VENEZUELA   BARBADOS
        TRINIDAD AND TOBAGO
        GUYANA
COLOMBIA   SURINAM

ECUADOR

PERU

BRAZIL

BOLIVIA

PARAGUAY

URUGUAY

ARGENTINA

CHILE

23.24

NORWAY SWEDEN

IRELAND
UNITED
KINGDOM

DENMARK

POLA

NETH.   W   E
BELG.   GERMANY
        LUX.
                        CZECHOSL.
FRANCE   AUSTRIA   HUN
        SWITZ.
PORTUGAL   YUGO

SPAIN   ITALY

0.48

MOROCCO

TUNISIA

ALGERIA

MAURITANIA   MALI   NIGER

SENEGAL
GAMBIA
        GUINEA
                UPPER
                VOLTA
SIERRA LEONE IVORY GHANA BENIN NIGERIA
        COAST TOGO
LIBERIA

                        CAMEROON
EQUATORIAL GUINEA
                        GABON
                        CONGO

Gold

**Official gold holdings February 1978
in millions of fine troy ounces
(approx. 32.1 oz = 1 kilogram)**

each 10 million (figures rounded)
5.1 — 10 million
1.1 — 5 million
1 million ounces and below

Extreme range: USA 277 million
               Mauritius 9000

**Identified private hoarding of gold 1968-78
millions of fine troy ounces**

below 1 million   *(notably France 202 million,
                  India 117 million*
above 1 million   *W. Germany 32 million,
                  USA 16.5 million)*

**Gold production 1978
millions of troy ounces**

over 20 million
10.1 — 20 million
1.1 — 10 million
1 million and below

**Gold bullion movements 1978
millions of fine troy ounces**

→ Major gold exports from producing countries
→ European distribution
→ Net sales from monetary stocks

US$

200

180

160

140

120

100

80

60

40

38.56

30

**Free market
price of gold
in US$**

**Annual
average
1968-79**

1980 high (to March) 835.00

1979 304.98

193.29

159.13 161.05

147.71

124.83

97.17

58.13

41.09 35.94 40.80

1968 1970 1972 1974 1976 1978

*Source: Consolidated Goldfields, Gold, 1979
J. L. Scherer ed. USSR Facts and Figures Annual,
Florida 1978*

inset

CYPRUS
SYRIA
LEBANON
ISRAEL
IRAQ
JORDAN
SAUDI
ARABIA

0.1

UNION OF SOVIET SOCIALIST REPUBLICS

5.59

MONGOLIA

TURKEY
inset
SYRIA
LEBANON
ISRAEL
IRAQ

IRAN

AFGHANISTAN

CHINA

N
S KOREA

JAPAN

0.1

0.87

YPT

KUWAIT

PAKISTAN

NEPAL
BHUTAN

TAIWAN

HONG KONG

SAUDI
ARABIA

BAHRAIN
QATAR
U.A.E.

OMAN

JDAN

N
YEMEN

S
YEMEN

0.32

INDIA

B-
DESH

BURMA

Burma Laos
Vietnam combined

THAILAND
LAOS
KAM

VIETNAM

PHILIPPINES

ETHIOPIA

SOMALIA

SRI LANKA

UGANDA
KENYA

MALAYSIA

W

SINGAPORE

TANZANIA

BIA
MALAWI

MADAGASCAR

ABWE

MOZAMBIQUE

S

INDONESIA

PAPUA
NEW GUINEA

Growth/decline in relative value between 1970 and 1979

Growth

over 25% growth

0 — 25% growth

Decline

0 — 25% decline

over 25% decline

Extreme range: Switzerland 89.8% growth — Italy 50.9% decline

Source: Morgan Guaranty Trust, World Financial Markets, January 1980

The Major Currencies

AUSTRALIA

NEW ZEALAND

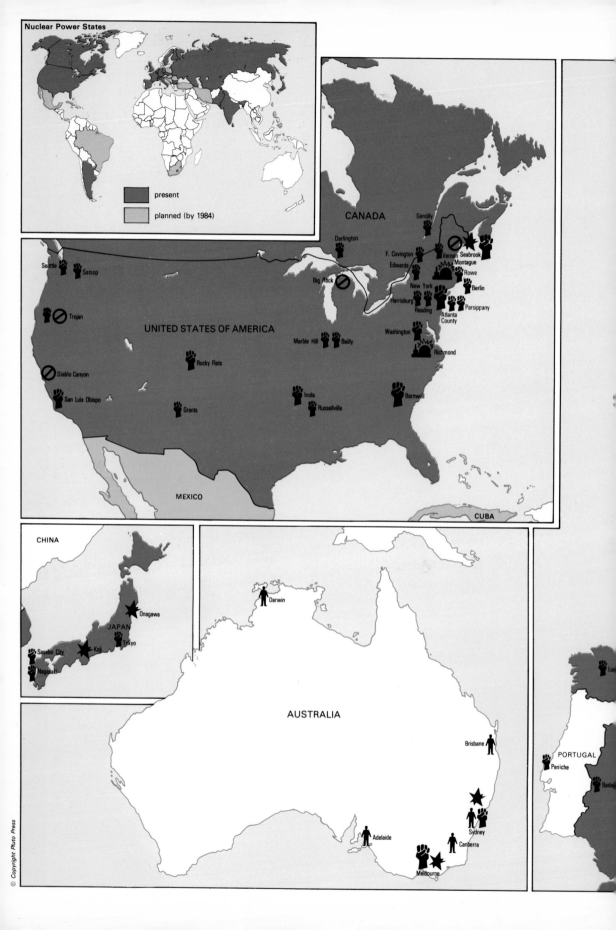

Nuclear Power States

present

planned (by 1984)

CANADA

Gentilly

Darlington

F. Covington
Edwards

Vernon Seabrook
Montague
Rowe

Big Rock

New York   Berlin
Harrisburg
Reading   Parsippany
Atlanta
County

Washington

Richmond

Seattle   Satsop

Trojan

UNITED STATES OF AMERICA

Marble Hill   Bailly

Diablo Canyon

Rocky Flats

San Luis Obispo

Grants

Inola
Russellville

Barnwell

MEXICO

CUBA

CHINA

JAPAN

Onagawa

Sasebo City   Koji   Tokyo

Nagasaki

Darwin

AUSTRALIA

Brisbane

Sydney

Canberra

Adelaide

Melbourne

PORTUGAL

Peniche

Badaj

Lu

© Copyright Pluto Press

60. Nuclear Power No Thanks

Protests against nuclear power and mining and transport of nuclear material: to early 1980

- strikes
- occupations
- sabotage
- serious battles with the police

demonstrations
- one
- two
- three or more

Nuclear power states
- present
- planned (by 1984)

Source: Press reports
Keesings Contemporary Archives
Anna Gyorgy and friends,
No Nukes: Everyone's Guide to Nuclear Power, 1979

NORWAY

SWEDEN

FINLAND

DENMARK

UNION OF SOVIET SOCIALIST REPUBLICS

POLAND

EAST GERMANY

NETHERLANDS

BELGIUM

WEST GERMANY

CZECHOSLOVAKIA

UNITED KINGDOM

FRANCE

SWITZ.

AUSTRIA

YUGOSLAVIA

ITALY

ALBANIA

GREECE

Helsinki

Stockholm

Goteborg

Gyllingnaes

Barsebaeck

Hojstrup

Brokdorf

Orkney Is

Torness

Glasgow
Edinburgh
Loch Doon
Barrow
Windscale
Hartlepool
Eysham
Liverpool
Capenhurst
London
Dungeness

Bassette
Esenshamm
Gorleben
Hanover
Almelo
Gronau
Kalkar
Grohnde
Borssele
Bonn
Aachen
Zwentendorf

La Hague
Cherbourg
Dieppe
Flammanville
Gravelines

Paris
Thionville
Nogent-sur-Seine
Chinon
Whyl
Kaiseraugst
Leibstadt
Lucens
Geneva
Goesgen
Fessenheim
Lons-le-Saunier
Creys-Malville
Bugey
Milan

Brennilis
Plogoff

Bilbao
Munguia
San Sebastian
Vitoria
Pamplona
Soria
Madrid

Marnac
Valance d'Agen
Pierrelatte
Lodève
Verfeil
Cruas
Tricostin
Avignon
Grenoble
Marseilles
Toulon
Seyne-sur-Mer

Capalbio
Montalto di Castro
Molise

Asco
Barcelona
Valencia

CANADA
Quebec

UNITED STATES OF AMERICA
Black Muslims

Mexican Americans

MEXICO
BAHAMAS
CUBA
JAMAICA
HAITI DOMINICAN REPUBLIC
PUERTO RICO
Puerto Rico
GUATEMALA
HONDURAS
EL SALVADOR
NICARAGUA
COSTA RICA
GRENADA
BARBADOS
TRINIDAD AND TOBAGO
Canal Zone
VENEZUELA
GUYANA
PANAMA
SURINAM
COLOMBIA
ECUADOR
PERU
BRAZIL
BOLIVIA
PARAGUAY
URUGUAY
ARGENTINA
CHILE

NORWAY
SWEDEN
FINLAND
Irish Republicans
Scotland
DENMARK
IRELAND
UNITED KINGDOM
Friesland
Wales
NETH
Flemings
POLAND
W E GERMANY
Walloons
LUX
CZECHOSLOVAKIA
Brittany
Alsace-Lorraine
FRANCE
AUST
HUNGARY
Galicia
SWITZ
Slovenes
South Tirol
Croats
YUGOSLAVIA
Basques
Friuli
Bosnian Mushms
Occitanie
ITALY
Albanians
SPAIN
Catalans
Corsica
ALBANIA
Andalusia
Sardinians
Valencia

Madeiras
Kabyls
TUNISIA
Canaries
MOROCCO
ALGERIA
West Saharans
(POLISARIO)
MAURITANIA
SENEGAL
MALI
NIGER
GAMBIA
UPPER VOLTA
NIGERIA
GUINEA
IVORY COAST
GHANA
BENIN
Borno
SIERRA LEONE
TOGO
Ex. Br. T.
LIBERIA
Ibo
CAMEROON
Ewe
GABON
Yoruba
Ibibio
Cabinda
Cameroons
AN
NA
Ovimbundu

Separatist, regionalist and irridentist
movements late 1970s

separatist movements
active   dormant

regionalist movements
active   dormant

irridentist movements
active   dormant

active area

Source: G. Ashworth ed., Case Studies on Human Rights
and Fundamental Freedoms, Vols. I-V, 1975-76
World Minorities, Vols. I and II, 1977
Minority Rights Group
B. Crozier, Annual of Power and Conflict, 1975-76 •
Keesings Contemporary Archives
Press reports

inset 1

The Case of the Kurds

TURKEY

SYRIA

IRAQ

IRAN

UNION OF SOVIET SOCIALIST REPUBLICS

see map 62

MONGOLIA

inset 1

TURKEY

CYPRUS
LHANON
ISRAEL
YPT
JORDAN

inset 2

SAUDI
ARABIA

QATAR
U.A.E.
OMAN

IRAN

AFGHANISTAN

Arabs

Pathans

PAKISTAN

Baluchis

KUWAIT

CHINA

Kashmir

Tibet

Nagaland

Kachins

Shans

NEPAL

BURMA

Mizoram

Chakmas

BANGLADESH

Karens

Meo

THAILAND

LAOS

KAM

VIETNAM

TAIWAN   Taiwanese

HONG KONG

PHILIPPINES

INDIA

inset 3

UDAN

YEMEN   S
YEMEN

DJIBOUTI

ETHIOPIA

SOMALIA

KENYA

Somalis

UGANDA

RWANDA   Hutu

TANZANIA

COMOROS

MALAWI

ABWE

MOZAMBIQUE

MADAGASCAR

Tamilnad

Tamils
SRI LANKA

Muslim Malays

Sabah

Sarawak

MALAYSIA

SINGAPORE

South
Molucca

INDONESIA

East Timor

Papuans

PAPUA
NEW GUINEA

AUSTRALIA

inset 2

TURKEY

Turks

Greek

SYRIA

IRAQ

Maronites

ISRAEL

Palestinians

JORDAN

SAUDI
ARABIA

inset 3

N
YEMEN   S
YEMEN

Eritrea

Somalis

Tigre

Somalis

ETHIOPIA

Harar &
Wollo

SOMALIA

NEW
ZEALAND

N   KOREA   JAPAN
S

East Siberian Sea

Laptev Sea

Ukta

R Kolyma

R Indigirka

R Lena

YAKUT

Petropavlosk-Kamchatskiy

R Aldan

Yakutsk

Sea of Okhotsk

Lower Tunguska

Stony Tunguska

JEWS to Jewish Autonomous Oblast

R Amur

BURYAT

Birobidjan
Blagoveshchensk
Khabarovsk

L Baykal

Irkutsk   Ulan-Ude

Vladivostok

Kyzyl
TUVA

SAAMI
ESTONIANS
LATVIANS
LITHS
KARELS
BYELO-
RUSSIANS
UKRAINIANS
KOMI
KHANTY
MANSI
YAKUTS
R U S S I A N S
BASHKIRS
KAZAKHS
BURYATS
BURYATS
GEORGIANS
ARMENIANS
JEWS
KAZAKHS
TURKMEN   KAZAKHS
TURKMEN   UZBEKS KIRGIZ
TADZHIKS

onstrations

how trials

n nationalism

d prison camps

tals

● Balts	● Paleo-Asiatics
○ Caucasians	● Slavs
● Finno-Ugrians	● Turkic
● Iranians	○ sparsely
● Mongols	populated

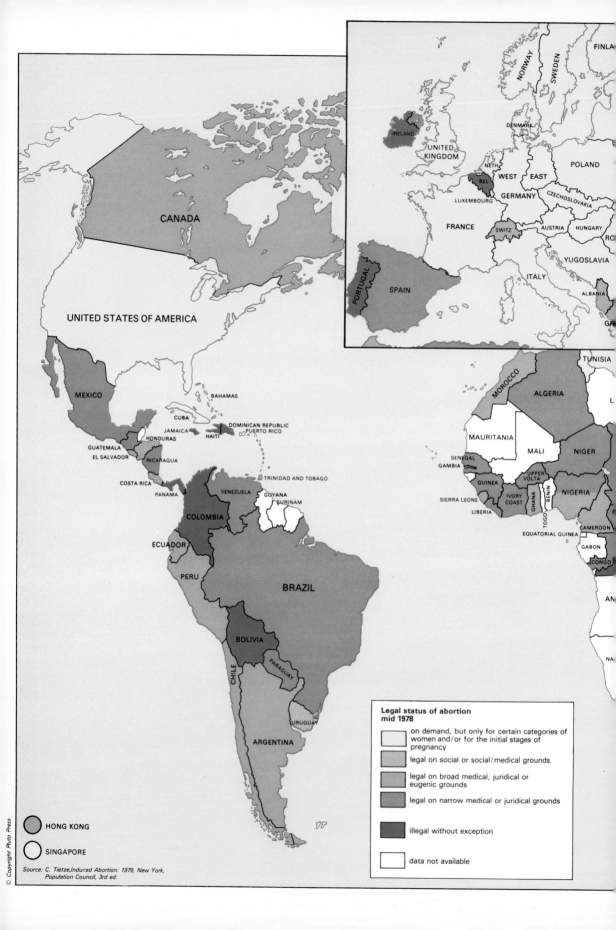

CANADA

UNITED STATES OF AMERICA

MEXICO

BAHAMAS

CUBA

JAMAICA
HONDURAS
GUATEMALA
EL SALVADOR
NICARAGUA
COSTA RICA
PANAMA

DOMINICAN REPUBLIC
PUERTO RICO
HAITI

TRINIDAD AND TOBAGO

VENEZUELA
GUYANA
SURINAM

COLOMBIA

ECUADOR

PERU

BRAZIL

BOLIVIA

PARAGUAY

CHILE

URUGUAY

ARGENTINA

NORWAY
SWEDEN
FINLA

DENMARK

IRELAND
UNITED KINGDOM

NETH
BEL
LUXEMBOURG
WEST EAST
GERMANY

POLAND

CZECHOSLOVAKIA

FRANCE
SWITZ
AUSTRIA
HUNGARY
RO

PORTUGAL
SPAIN

ITALY

YUGOSLAVIA

ALBANIA

GR

TUNISIA

MOROCCO
ALGERIA
L

MAURITANIA
MALI
NIGER

SENEGAL
GAMBIA
GUINEA
UPPER
VOLTA
BENIN
NIGERIA

SIERRA LEONE
LIBERIA
IVORY
COAST
GHANA
TOGO

CAMEROON

EQUATORIAL GUINEA

GABON
CONGO

AN

NA

**Legal status of abortion
mid 1978**

on demand, but only for certain categories of
women and/or for the initial stages of
pregnancy

legal on social or social/medical grounds

legal on broad medical, juridical or
eugenic grounds

legal on narrow medical or juridical grounds

illegal without exception

data not available

HONG KONG

SINGAPORE

Source: C. Tietze, Induced Abortion: 1979, New York,
Population Council, 3rd ed.

inset

TURKEY

CYPRUS

SYRIA

LEBANON

ISRAEL

IRAQ

EGYPT

JORDAN

SAUDI ARABIA

UNION OF SOVIET SOCIALIST REPUBLICS

MONGOLIA

JAPAN

N KOREA
S

CHINA

TURKEY

PRUS

SYRIA

BANON

ISRAEL

IRAQ

IRAN

AFGHANISTAN

PAKISTAN

inset

PT

QATAR

UAE

KUWAIT

SAUDI ARABIA

OMAN

DAN

N YEMEN

S YEMEN

ETHIOPIA

SOMALIA

UGANDA

KENYA

TANZANIA

MALAWI

MADAGASCAR

ABWE

MOZAMBIQUE

S

NEPAL

BHUTAN

INDIA

B-
DESH

BURMA

LAOS

THAILAND

KAM

VIETNAM

SRI LANKA

TAIWAN

PHILIPPINES

MALAYSIA

INDONESIA

PAPUA
NEW
GUINEA

AUSTRALIA

NEW ZEALAND

Changes in Abortion 1963-78

liberal policy or law before 1963

significant change to
more liberal law or policy

significant change to
more restrictive law or policy

no significant change, or data not available

FIJI
HONG KONG
PAPUA NEW GUINEA
SINGAPORE
WESTERN SAMOA

CANADA

UNITED STATES
OF AMERICA

MEXICO

BAHAMAS

CUBA

BELIZE   JAMAICA
GUATEMALA   NICARAGUA   HAITI
EL SALVADOR   DOMINICAN REPUBLIC
HONDURAS   PUERTO RICO
COSTA RICA   BARBADOS
PANAMA   TRINIDAD AND TOBAGO

VENEZUELA
GUYANA
COLOMBIA   SURINAM

ECUADOR

PERU
BRAZIL

BOLIVIA

PARAGUAY

URUGUAY

CHILE   ARGENTINA

NORWAY   SWEDEN   FINLAND

DENMARK

IRELAND   UNITED
          KINGDOM
NETH.   GERMANY
BEL.   POLAND
          SWITZ.   CZECHOSLOVAKIA
FRANCE
          AUSTRIA   HUNGARY
PORTUGAL   YUGOSLAVIA
SPAIN   ITALY
                    ALBANIA

U.N.
SOVIET
REP.

RO

GRE

TUNISIA

MOROCCO   ALGERIA

MAURITANIA   MALI   NIGER

CAPE VERDE
          SENEGAL
GAMBIA
GUINEA-BISSAU   UPPER
          GUINEA   VOLTA
SIERRA LEONE   IVORY   NIGERIA
          COAST   GHANA   BENIN
LIBERIA   TOGO
                    CAMEROON
EQUATORIAL GUINEA
                    GABON
                    CONG

Major student disruptions
1968-69

★ site of disruption

Source: Press reports
Keesing's Contemporary Archives, 1968-69
and various books

**Student enrolment at universities
and equivalent institutions
1968 or nearest year**

under 10,000

10,000 - 200,000

200,000 - 500,000

over 500,000

data not available

Source: UNESCO Statistical Yearbooks 1972, 1975

UNION OF SOVIET SOCIALIST REPUBLICS

MONGOLIA

TURKEY

CYPRUS
SYRIA
ISRAEL
IRAQ
IRAN

EGYPT
KUWAIT
QATAR
UAE
OMAN

SAUDI
ARABIA

SUDAN

N
YEMEN
S
YEMEN
DJIBOUTI

ETHIOPIA

SOMALIA

UGANDA

KENYA

TANZANIA

COMOROS

MALAWI

MOZAMBIQUE

MADAGASCAR

ZIMBABWE

AFGHANISTAN

PAKISTAN

NEPAL
BHUTAN

INDIA

E.PAKISTAN

BURMA

SRI LANKA

CHINA

MONGOLIA

N KOREA

JAPAN

TAIWAN

LAOS

THAILAND

VIETNAM

KAM

PHILIPPINES

BRUNEI

MALAYSIA

SINGAPORE

INDONESIA

PAPUA
NEW GUINEA

AUSTRALIA

NEW
ZEALAND

CANADA

UNITED STATES OF AMERICA

BERMUDA

inset

PORTUGAL

SPAIN

Madrid

Lisbon

FRANCE

ICELAND

ALGERIA

NORWAY

IRELAND

UNITED KINGDOM

DENMARK

NETH BEL

W E GERMANY

CZ

inset

PORTUGAL

SPAIN

FRANCE

SW

ITALY

YUG

AL

MEXICO

BAHAMAS

CUBA

JAMAICA

HAITI

DOMINICAN REPUBLIC

PUERTO RICO

HONDURAS

GUATEMALA

EL SALVADOR

NICARAGUA

Managua

BARBADOS

GRENADA

PANAMA

COSTA RICA

TRINIDAD AND TOBAGO

VENEZUELA

ECUADOR

COLOMBIA

GUYANA

SURINAM

PERU

BRAZIL

BOLIVIA

PARAGUAY

CHILE

Santiago

URUGUAY

Buenos Aires

ARGENTINA

MOROCCO

ALGERIA

TUNISIA

L

MAURITANIA

MALI

NIGER

GAMBIA

SENEGAL

GUINEA

UPPER VOLTA

NIGERIA

SIERRA LEONE

IVORY COAST

Accra

GHANA

TOGO

BENIN

Lagos

Monrovia

LIBERIA

CAMEROON

EQUATORIAL GUINEA

GABON

CONG

AN

NAM

MAURITIUS
Port Louis

★ site of urban upheaval

Widespread urban upheaval or strike
action involving major industrial
centres in the 1970s

| once | twice | three times | four or more times |

change in government or government policy
resulting from major urban upheaval

*Source: Keesings Contemporary Archives
Press reports*

© *Copyright Pluto Press*

The States of the World

Sovereign states and dependent territories referred to in this atlas
*Dependent territories

Afghanistan	Democratic Republic of Afghánistán
Albania	Republika Popullore Socialiste e Shqipërisë
Algeria	El Djemhouria El Djazaïria Eddemokratia Echaabia
Andorra	Les Vallées d'Andorra
	Valls d'Andorra
Angola	Angola
Antigua	Antigua
Argentina	República Argentina
Australia	Australia
Austria	Republik Österreich
Bahamas	The Commonwealth of the Bahamas*
Bahrain	Bahrain
Bangladesh	People's Republic of Bangladesh
Barbados	Barbados
Belgium	Royaume de Belgique
	Koninkrijk België
Belize	Belize*
Benin	République Populaire du Benin
Bermuda	Bermuda*
Bhutan	Druk-yul
Bolivia	República de Bolivia
Botswana	Botswana
Brazil	República Federativa do Brasil
Brunei	Brunei
Bulgaria	Narodna Republika Bulgaria
Burma	Pyidaungsu Socialist Thammada Myanma Naingngandaw
Burundi	Burundi
Cambodia *see* **Kampuchea**	
Cameroon	République Unie du Cameroun
Canada	Canada
Cape Verde	República de Cabo Verde
Cayman Islands	Cayman Islands*
Central African Republic	Central African Republic
Chad	République du Tchad
Chile	República de Chile
China	Zhonghua Renmin Gonghe Guo (People's Republic of China)
Colombia	República de Colombia
Comoros	Etat Comorien
Congo	République Populaire du Congo
Costa Rica	República de Costa Rica
Cuba	República de Cuba
Cyprus	Kypriaki Dimokratia
	Kibris Cumhuriyeti
Czechoslovakia	Ceskoslovenská Socialistická Republika
Denmark	Kongeriget Danmark
Djibouti	Republic of Djibouti
Dominica	Commonwealth of Dominica
Dominican Republic	República Dominicana
Ecuador	República del Ecuador
Egypt	Arab Republic of Egypt
El Salvador	República de El Salvador

Equatorial Guinea	República de Guinea Ecuatorial
Ethiopia	Ethiopia
Falkland Islands	Falklands Islands and Dependencies*
Fiji	Fiji
Finland	Suomen Tasavalta
	Republiken Finland
France	République Française
French Guiana	Guyane Française*
Gabon	République Gabonaise
Gambia	The Gambia
Guadeloupe	Guadeloupe*
Germany, East	Deutsche Demokratische Republik
	(German Democratic Republic)
Germany, West	Bundesrepublik Deutschland
	(Federal Republic of Germany)
Ghana	Ghana
Gilbert Islands *see* Kiribati	
Greece	Elliniki Dimokratia
Greenland	Grønland*
Grenada	Grenada
Guatemala	República de Guatemala
Guinea	République Populaire at Révolutionnaire de
	Guinée
Guinea-Bissau	Guinea-Bissau
Guyana	Guyana
Haiti	République d'Haiti
Honduras	República de Honduras
Hong Kong	Hong Kong*
Hungary	Magyar Népköztársaság
Iceland	Lýðveldið Ísland
India	Bharat
Indonesia	Republik Indonesia
Iran	Jumhouriy Islamiy Irân
	Islamic Republic of Iran
Iraq	al Jumhouriya al 'Iraqia
Ireland	Éire
Israel	Medinat Israel
	(State of Israel)
Italy	Repubblica Italiana
Ivory Coast	République de Côte d'Ivoire
Jamaica	Jamaica
Japan	Nippon (or Nihon)
Jordan	Al Mamlaka al Urduniya al Hashemiyah
	(The Hashemite Kingdom of Jordan)
Kampuchea	Democratic Kampuchea (formerly Cambodia)
Kenya	Djumhuri ya Kenya
Kiribati	Kiribati (formerly Gilbert Islands)
Korea, North	Chosun Minchu-chui Inmin Konghwa-guk
Korea, South	Han Kook
Kuwait	Dowlat al Kuwait
Laos	Laos
Lebanon	al-Jumhouriya al-Lubnaniya
Lesotho	Lesotho
Liberia	Liberia
Libya	Al-Jamahirayah Al-Arabiya
	Al Libya Al Shabiya Al-Ishtirakiya
	(Socialist People's Libyan Arab Jamahiriyah)

Liechtenstein	Liechenstein
Luxembourg	Grand-Duché de Luxembourg
Madagascar	The Democratic Republic of Madagascar
Malawi	Malawi
Malaysia	Malaysia
Maldives	Republic of Maldives
Mali	République du Mali
Malta	Republika Ta Malta
Martinique	Martinique*
Mauritania	République Islamique de Mauritanie
Mauritius	Mauritius
Mexico	Estados Unidos Mexicanos
Monaco	Monaco
Mongolia	Bügd Nayramdakh Mongol Ard Uls (Mongolian People's Republic)
Morocco	al-Mamlaka al-Maghrebia
Mozambique	The People's Republic of Mozambique
Namibia	South-West Africa* Suidwes-Afrika*
Nauru	Nauru
Nepal	Népal
Netherlands	Koninkrijk de Nederlanden
New Hebrides *see* **Vanuatu Republic**	
New Zealand	New Zealand
Nicaragua	República de Nicaragua
Niger	République du Niger
Nigeria	Federal Republic of Nigeria
Norway	Kongeriket Norge
Oman	Saltanat Oman
Pakistan	Islamic Republic of Pakistan
Panama	República de Panamá
Papua New Guinea	Papua New Guinea
Paraguay	República del Paraguay
Peru	República del Perú
Philippines	República de Filipinas Republika ñg Pilipinas
Poland	Polska Rzeczpospolita Ludowa
Portugal	República Portuguesa
Puerto Rico	Puerto Rico*
Qatar	State of Qatar
Reunion	La Réunion*
Rhodesia *see* **Zimbabwe**	
Romania	Republica Socialistă România
Rwanda	Rwanda
St Christopher (St Kitts)-Nevis-Anguilla	St Christopher (St Kitts)-Nevis-Anguilla*
St Lucia	St Lucia*
St Vincent	St Vincent and the Grenadines*
San Marino	Repubblica di San Marino
Sao Tome and Principe	São Tomé e Principe
Saudi Arabia	al-Mamlaka al-'Arabiya as-Sa'udiya
Senegal	République du Sénégal
Seychelles	Seychelles
Sierra Leone	Sierra Leone
Singapore	Republic of Singapore
Solomon Islands	Solomon Islands
Somalia	Al-Jumhouriya As-Somaliya Al-Democradia (Somali Democratic Republic)

South Africa	Republiek van Suid-Afrika
	Republic of South Africa
South-West Africa *see* **Namibia**	
Spain	Estado Español
Sri Lanka	Sri Lanka
Sudan	Jamhuryat es-Sudan Al Democratia
	(The Democratic Republic of the Sudan)
Surinam	Suriname
Swaziland	Swaziland
Sweden	Konungariket Sverige
Switzerland	Suisse
	Svizzera
	Schweiz
Syria	al-Jamhouriya al Arabia as-Souriya
Taiwan	Republic of China
Tanzania	United Republic of Tanzania
Thailand	Prathes Thai
	Muang-Thai
Togo	République Togolaise
Tonga	Tonga (Friendly Islands)
Trinidad and Tobago	Trinidad and Tobago
Tunisia	Al-Djoumhouria Attunusia
Turkey	Türkiye Cumhuriyeti
Tuvalu	Tuvalu
Uganda	Uganda
Union of Soviet Socialist Republics (USSR)	Soyuz Sovyetskikh Sotsialisticheskikh Respublik
United Arab Emirates	United Arab Emirates
United Kingdom	United Kingdom of Great Britain and Northern Ireland
United States of America (USA)	United States of America
Upper Volta	République de Haute-Volta
Uruguay	República Oriental del Uruguay
Vanuatu Republic	Vanuatu Republic (formerly New Hebrides)
Vatican City	Vatican City State
Venezuela	República de Venezuela
Vietnam	Công Hòa Xã Hôi Chu Nghĩa Viêt Nam
	(The Socialist Republic of Vietnam)
Virgin Islands (British)	British Virgin Islands
Western Samoa	Samoa i Sisifo
Yemen, North	al Jamhuriya al Arabiya al Yamaniya
	(Yemen Arab Republic)
Yemen, South	Jumhurijah al-Yemen al Dimuqratiyah al Sha'abijah
	The People's Democratic Republic of Yemen
Yugoslavia	Socijalisticka Federativna Republika Jugoslavija
	(Socialist Federal Republic of Yugoslavia)
Zaire	République du Zaïre
Zambia	Zambia
Zimbabwe	Zimbabwe

Source: Statesman's Yearbook 1980–81, with amendments indicated by changed circumstances, e.g. Vanuatu, Iran; or by different interpretations of unchanged circumstances, e.g. Namibia

Notes to the Maps

This map shows the proliferation of states since 1945, when much of the world was still run from Europe. A further state, Vanuatu (the New Hebrides), became independent in July 1980, and the existence of powerful separatist movements (see *Map 61: Nationalism Against the Nation State*) suggests that the process of proliferation is still far from over.

A list of the many states with a population of less than a million is given on the map. For comparison, the estimated population of China in 1979 was 850 million, and that of India in 1979, 605 million.

Sovereign states are those that are generally accepted as such by other sovereign states and by international agencies. Thus Taiwan is included, although the governments of both China and Taiwan continue to insist that the island is an integral part of China. Similarly, both the Transkei and the Ukraine are excluded: the first is recognized only by South Africa, and the second, while recognized by the UN, is not deemed independent by any member state. In addition, there are border regions held by one sovereign state and claimed by another. The most notable example is Kashmir, which though incorporated into India is still claimed by Pakistan. No judgement is made on such disputes within this atlas and all states and boundaries conform to those given in *The Times Atlas of the World.*

The two Germanies are shown as new states because neither existed in its present form before 1945. It would have been even more misleading to have shown them as both existing, independently sovereign, in 1945.

Although Greenland is named to distinguish it from the neighbouring Canadian land mass, it is constitutionally part of Denmark. Likewise, Guadeloupe and Martinique, in the Caribbean, are constitutionally part of France.

Some longstanding European statelets, shown as insets on the left of the map, allow their foreign affairs to be controlled by powerful neighbours. They are not really states in the accepted sense at all.

This map compares the populations of the world's states in 1979 and gives their annual average growth rate during the seventies.

Population is shown by a graphic distortion which preserves the geographical relationship between states. What emerges is an idea of how very different the world would look if the size of each state corresponded to its population. States with less than a million inhabitants have been excluded. A list of these is given on *Map 2: The Proliferation of States.*

Population growth rates are shown in colour. On current trends, a map of this kind produced year after year would show a marked and continuing decrease in the size of the rich states relative to the rest.

For other graphically distorted maps, which give a different view of the world, see for example *Map 23: National Income* or *Map 26: Government Income.*

For many states, population figures are no better than inspired guesses. In the US, for example, the existence of a large illegal immigrant society, officially estimated at between two and twelve million (see note to *Map 38: The Flight to Work*) is among the many factors in the widely recognized under-recording of population. In others, recording and non-recording of population forms part of the political tussle between its constituent parts — as between the states in Nigeria. In yet others there are simply no provisions for a separate census administration and population figures are supplied by officials engaged in other, seemingly more pressing, business and who have not necessarily been appointed for their numeracy.

4. The State Invades Antarctica

These four maps show the gathering invasion by the state system of the last large unpossessed land mass. They show Antarctica's potential mineral wealth, which states are claimants to its territory, and where each of those claimants has set up scientific stations. One US settlement, the Amundsen—Scott base at the South Pole, is at the meeting point of all the territorial claims in the continent, as if to underline the USA's refusal to recognize them.

Antarctica is rich in resources. It is already a major source of protein in the form of fish, whale meat and increasingly, krill (the many species of oceanic shrimp which constitute the basic food of whales). It holds promise of being a major source of the many minerals already mined in Southern Africa, Australia and South America with which Antarctica shares a common geological past. It is suspected of being rich in mineral oil and gas deposits. It also harbours 70 per cent of the world's fresh water which, in the form of ice, could be detached, towed and made available to the world's arid zones.

Antarctica is attractive in other ways. Scientifically, it is an isolated, relatively clean place from which to monitor global climatic conditions and changes, or levels of atmospheric pollution. It is also a useful base for research into human adaptability to extreme cold and dryness. Its remoteness is causing it to be viewed as a potential nuclear dustbin, able to absorb the radioactive waste that is too dangerous to store or to hide in the populated areas of the world. Militarily, it is attractive for its relative distance from likely theatres of war and its closeness to the only sea link between the Pacific, Atlantic and Indian Oceans other than the vulnerable Suez and Panama Canals.

5. The State Invades the Sea

'If a new and broadly accepted law of the sea does not emerge through international agreement, we face the prospect of each state determining its own view, with ever-widening claims to ocean space and resources. The acceptance of such a situation, favouring as it would power at the expense of justice, and risking unforeseeable possibilities of conflict, is unthinkable.' Kurt Waldheim, Secretary General, opening the sixth annual session of the Third United Nations Conference on the Law of the Sea, 15 May 1979.

This map shows how an extension of national jurisdiction to 200 nautical miles off all coasts, including those of islands, could affect as much as one-third of the sea area that covers some 70 per cent of the globe. Most littoral states have already claimed an Exclusive Economic Zone (EEZ) of 200 miles and, in some cases, the greater riches of the continental shelf have led to claims of 350 miles or more.

The many areas where EEZs overlap are areas of potential conflict. Some of these have caused disputes not yet resolved, and they are shown on the map. Where agreements have been reached (as between Britain and France for example) they have not been included.

The map also shows the areas of major fishing disputes between states, some of which date from pre-EEZ times. Such disputes, and similar disputes concerning sea-bed and undersea-bed resources, can only be fuelled by the new claims to hitherto free resources.

In the process of establishing and extending EEZs, small island territories have a special value. Some zones shown on the map have no apparent territorial source. This is because the islands which extend these EEZs are too small to show up on a map of this scale.

6. Invasions of the Sky

No state has so far claimed territorial rights to the stratosphere, and very few have invaded any part of it with people or materials. But the drive to do so is strong. By the end of the seventies, the pattern of satellite launches had become relatively fixed from year to year and this illustration gives an impressionistic view of launches made in 1978.

Two important and menacing developments took place in that year: the launching of the first hunter-killer satellite, and the contamination of a part of the earth's surface with radioactive debris from a satellite crash.

The satellite illustrated in the bottom right-hand corner of the map is one launched by the European Space Agency, which has eleven member states, whose shares range from Denmark's 2.19 per cent to West Germany's 25 per cent.

The relatively large number of Russian launches reflects the short life span of their satellites which, in contrast to US satellites, is usually measured in days rather than months.

It has been estimated that to the end of the seventies there have been roughly 2,000 launches, through which more than 11,300 man-made objects have been put into space: satellites, rockets, nose cones, shields, capsules and the like, along with fragments from the various space shots that went wrong.

Satellite tracking stations on earth have been overwhelmingly American. However, these are now becoming redundant as new techniques permit surveillance from fixed satellites, without the risk and dependence upon foreign governments and their citizens.

7. Foreign Military Presence

This map records all foreign air, land and sea bases at the end of the seventies. By its very nature, the subject is one on which those who have the information are most reluctant to part with it. It is also one in which abrupt changes in political alignment may lead to equally abrupt rearrangements of the bases which express and support them.

As a whole, the map shows that the global disposition of military forces not only reflects interstate alliances and old imperial interests, but also the fundamental confrontation between Western and Soviet bloc states.

Army bases are distinguished according to whether troops are stationed there primarily for fighting purposes or primarily for training, advisory or surveillance ones. Combat forces are divided into major and minor presences, namely, large self-contained forces organized as divisions of 10,000 or more (and occasionally, as in the case of Britain, 8,500 or more) and smaller forces of battalion strength or more.

It has been impossible to locate the precise sites of many foreign bases other than those of the Americans. Lack of information has also made it impossible to record the changes in tenancy of landing, refuelling and servicing facilities in the Middle East and the Horn of Africa, as Russians gave way to Americans in the last months of the seventies and the early months of 1980.

8. Military Spending

This map shows in colour, how much of each state's gross national product (GNP) is spent on military uses. Symbols are used to show the proportion of central government expenditure so employed. A regional summary is given in the inset map.

The source of these statistics is the US Arms Control and Development Agency, which tends to understate US arms expenditure (see the note to *Map 11: Arms for the Sake of the Profit*).

There is little correspondence between military spending and the nature of individual regimes. Many military regimes or regimes with a substantial military presence, as in Latin America for example, spend a relatively small proportion of their income on military purposes (see *Map 28: Military Government*). The financial cost of domestic repression over unarmed populations is small.

The real impulse to high military spending lies in global or regional confrontation between states. What the map shows overall is how much of the world's resources are devoted to unproductive preparations for war and to mutual destruction.

9. The Nuclear Club

This map shows the extent to which individual states are armed with deliverable nuclear weapons — on their own account or at the behest of an allied state.

A 'known nuclear weapons state' is one which has manufactured and exploded a nuclear weapon or other nuclear explosive device. A 'suspected nuclear weapons state' is one which is widely reputed to have constructed already, or to be able to construct within a very short time, several nuclear weapons. A 'near nuclear weapons state' is one which could develop this capability by the year 2000. An important component of this capability is the commissioning of a nuclear reactor, either for research or for the generation of electricity (see *Map 17: Nuclear Power*).

The danger in the proliferation of nuclear weapons has been underlined by Pakistan's public commitment to construct a nuclear weapon, despite considerable pressure from the main nuclear powers. This commitment is reportedly financed by Libya on the understanding that Libya would share in the result. And during the preparation of this atlas, Pakistan has leapt from being a rather distant candidate for the 'nuclear club' to being an imminent member.

10. Air Power

This map shows the comparative potency of individual states in conventional warfare. It uses the single but important index, numbers of combat aircraft. All naval and army combat aircraft are included, but not training, counter-insurgency and troop-carrying planes, or helicopters.

Numbers are by no means an invariable measure of potency. China's huge combat air force is seriously obsolescent; many of Egypt's aircraft, supplied by the Russians, are grounded for lack of spare parts; Iran's air force is increasingly understaffed and demoralized.

Yet the map provides the best comparison of potency in conventional warfare currently available. To have compared numbers of soldiers would have been to ignore the capacity of the weapons available to them, and this is often more material than the quantity of military personnel. Ownership of warships is limited to littoral states and is likely to be further influenced by the apparent vulnerability of coastal regions. As for land vehicles, it proved difficult to distinguish adequately between tanks and fighting vehicles; and among tanks, difficult to distinguish heavy, medium and light from one another.

11. Arms for the Sake of the Profit

This graphically distorted map shows the relative amounts spent by states on the purchase of foreign arms. Major arms exporters are distinguished from major external arms importers and, in the case of the latter, the major source of arms is shown in colour. The colour breakdown in the figures at the bottom of the map provides a regional summary of the size and source of arms imports.

The acquisition of weapons is an expensive business, and for those who are able to supply them, an extremely profitable one. Although even major arms suppliers, such as France and the United Kingdom, seem to dwindle beside the two giants in arms supply, the USA and the USSR, it does not follow that their trade is unimportant for them, or for their particular markets. Exports are, in fact, less crucial to the arms industry in the USA and USSR, which have huge domestic arms markets, than to states large parts of whose arms production is often ultimately dependent on the existence of export markets to supplement domestic ones.

Available statistics give different impressions of the USA's share of the arms market. The official US statistics which we have used, from the US Arms Control and Disarmament Agency, estimates the USA's share of world arms sales in 1976 at 39 per cent. While Tom Gervasi, in *Arsenal of Democracy* (New York, Grove Press 1977) attributes more than 50 per cent of such sales to the USA, and the *SIPRI Yearbook 1979*, 48 per cent.

The choice of major arms supplier is, for some states, not a static one. Since the statistics for this map were collected, for instance, both Egypt and Somalia have elected to buy the majority of their arms from the USA rather than the USSR.

This map is concerned solely with armed conflict between independent states in the seventies which involved uniformed personnel of the regular armed forces. It shows both the participants in such wars and the actual area of conflict. For internal armed conflict, see *Map 61: Nationalism Against the Nation State.*

Of course, the nature of such conflicts and their impact on the protagonists has differed enormously: from minor border clashes, as between Libya and Egypt, to the so-called Yom Kippur war in the Middle East, the wars between India and Pakistan and the long Vietnam war which was fought as well in both Kampuchea and Laos.

States are depicted as they were in early 1980; they may not have existed or existed in their current form at the time of some of the conflicts shown. Bangladesh was not an independent state during one of the wars between India and Pakistan. And it was the armed forces of Rhodesia that were engaged against Zambia and Mozambique before Zimbabwe was recognized as an independent state in 1980.

Thirteen minerals of generally accepted economic and strategic importance have been chosen to illustrate the disparity in the distribution of the world's mineral resources among states. Three of the most important minerals are dealt with elsewhere: in an inset map to *Map 15: Energy Power* (coal); *Map 16: Oil Power*; and *Map 59: Panic Stations* (gold). Of the minerals included in these two maps: antimony is used in the manufacture of batteries and, increasingly, as a flame retardant; and manganese is important not only as a steel hardening agent but also in the chemical industry.

Possession of a large quantity of a single important mineral does not necessarily convey a corresponding economic strength. In many instances, mines may be owned by foreign-based transnational corporations (see *Map 36: The Nationality of Transnationals*) which as far as possible dispose of resources in their own interests. Furthermore, market forces may so adjust the current value of particular minerals as to turn a major mine from a highly prized and profitable operation into a vulnerable, loss-making one. None the less, there are five states (shown in Map 14) whose abundance and diversity of mineral resources makes it appropriate to term them mineral powers: Australia, Canada, South Africa, the USA and the USSR.

In some states, the statistics for diamond production do not distinguish between gem and industrial stones. For this reason, the combined figure is given in all cases. South Africa dominates the international market in gem stones: partly through its own important share of world production; partly through its control of the Namibian mines; and not least because, through the Central Selling Organization, it commands an effective world monopoly to whose operations the USSR, amongst others, is party.

A reservation must be made with regard to the figures for chrome. During the period of UDI, from 1964 to 1980, some chrome mined in Zimbabwe, then Rhodesia, was almost certainly exported via South Africa and included in that country's statistics.

This map shows the relationship between each state's energy consumption and production. States with a small or large energy surplus (those which produce more than they consume) are contrasted with states which have a small or large energy deficit (those which consume more than they produce).

The existence of an energy deficiency helps to explain certain policies. The enormous dependence of Japan on imported sources of energy has led to the Japanese government committing itself to a doubling of nuclear power generating capacity within the next few years. (See *Map 17: Nuclear Power.*)

Since the statistics for this map were prepared, the exploitation of rich oil deposits has been substantially changing the ratios of energy pro-

12. States at War in the 1970s

13. Mineral Power

14. The World Mineral Powers

15. Energy Power

duction and consumption for some states: for instance, Mexico, Norway and the United Kingdom. However, this process has not affected the usefulness of the broad categories employed in the map.

Some comment on the statistics used is necessary:

Renewable energy sources, such as solar, tidal and wind power, which require advanced technology for their development, have been so neglected as to be considered negligible and are excluded by the source of the map, *UN World Energy Supplies 1973–77*. Traditional sources, such as wood and dung, are also excluded. Where their contribution is important, as in India and some African states, no accurate figures are available. Where such figures are available, as for some European states, their relative contribution is unimportant.

Production data are based on the production of coal, lignite, crude petroleum, natural gas, natural gas liquids, hydro- and nuclear electricity. Where peat is important as fuel, it is included.

Consumption data are based on the apparent consumption of coal, lignite, petroleum products, natural gas, hydro- and nuclear electricity. Coke, manufactured gas, and electricity traded internationally are considered to have been consumed by importing countries.

Comparison between coal and other sources of energy is based on calorific value. One metric ton of coal is equivalent to 1.47 metric tons of crude petroleum or 1.67 metric tons of natural gas liquid.

The steeply rising price of oil has caused renewed interest in the world's coal resources. Coal can be used as a substitute fuel for power stations and is itself a source of oil. The inset map compares coal production and consumption in all states where it is above 10 million metric tons a year.

16. Oil Power

This map compares the oil production and consumption of individual states where it amounts to more than 0.5 per cent of the world's total. Annual average rates of growth or decline are shown in colour and major oil movements, in proportion to their size, are shown in all cases where they are above 5 million metric tons.

The soaring price of oil during the seventies has given the major oil-exporting states enormous economic power. The Organization of Petroleum Exporting Countries (OPEC) first used its united weight in 1973. Since then, even those oil exporters which have remained outside the cartel, such as Mexico and the United Kingdom, have effectively accepted its leadership in setting prices. Saudi Arabia is by far the largest oil exporter in the world and among OPEC members it is by far the most influential. The United States has publicly and repeatedly pressed Saudi Arabia to use this influence to hold down oil prices. But fear of damaging the cartel and other regional political constraints have qualified Saudi Arabia's ability to do so.

The increasing dependence of the United States on imported oil has been a crucial factor in its persistently enormous trade deficit in the post war period. This has led to the depreciation of the US dollar against many currencies, the erosion of confidence in the dollar as a reserve currency, and an international monetary upheaval without precedent since the second world war. This upheaval is the subject of *Map 59: Panic Stations.*

At present the USSR is still a major oil exporter. But reliable estimates suggest that within a few years it will, like the USA, be an oil importer on an increasing scale. The economic and political consequences of a scramble by the two superpowers for scarce and costly oil supplies are unlikely to be comfortable.

17. Nuclear Power

Two major factors contribute to the current rush by states to develop nuclear power stations. First, growing energy deficits exacerbated by the rising price of oil, and second, the access that such programmes offer to the production of nuclear weapons (see *Map 10: The Nuclear Club*). There is no doubt that the latter is a significant inducement for some poor states, with a relatively low energy consumption, to undertake ambitious nuclear power programmes.

By 1978, 5.85 per cent of the world's total electricity generating power already came from nuclear power stations. This proportion will increase dramatically if all the power stations planned are put into operation.

Only nuclear power reactors likely to produce more than 20 megawatts (mW(e)) per year are included and the information on planned nuclear reactors is, of course, liable to rapid change.

For public response to the dangers of such programmes, see *Map 60: Nuclear Power No Thanks.*

18. Food Power

In this graphically distorted map, colour is used to show whether states have a small or large deficit in food trade. The size of each state is related to its share of world food trade in 1977; if a state is a net exporter, its size is determined by its share of world food exports; if a net importer, by its share of world food imports.

The main exporters of staple grains – the USA, Canada, Australia and Argentina – can use their food surplus as an instrument of considerable power. The US Secretary of State for Agriculture, Earl Butz, said in 1974, 'Food is a weapon. It is now one of the principal weapons in our negotiating kit.' In 1980, in response to the Russian invasion of Afghanistan, the USA embargoed all sales of grain to the USSR not already pledged by contract.

Some states may well show an overall surplus in food trade and yet be unable to nourish their populations at all adequately. Such surpluses are in many cases created by large exports of a single food or beverage commodity, especially coffee, cocoa, sugar and honey, or tropical fruits (see *Map 21: Dependence and Diversity*). Comparison should also be made with *Map 44: Our Daily Bread*. Colombia, a major coffee exporter, is shown here to have a substantial surplus in food trade. Yet the number of calories available per head of population is below requirement and there was a famine in Colombia in 1967. Africa's case is even more ironic. Here it is shown to have an overall surplus in food trade as a result of major exports of coffee, cocoa and tropical fruits. Yet it remains one of the world's most desperate areas of undernourishment and even starvation.

19. Industrial Power

This map shows the enormous discrepancies in industrial wealth, and the power associated with it, between a relatively small number, and the vast mass of the world's states. Canada, for example, with a population of 23 million has more industrial power than the whole of Africa and India combined. The map shows too, the enormous industrial dominance of the USA, although it is diminishing in relation to Japan and the main industrial states of Western Europe. (See also *Map 55: Industrial Droop* which shows the generally decreasing rates of industrial growth between the sixties and the seventies.)

In this map, as elsewhere in this atlas, the need for manageable bands of comparison produces a low band which contains considerable disparities. As an extreme example, the Central African Republic, with an industrial output of US$46 million per year in the mid-seventies is bracketed with Egypt, whose annual industrial output was US$4,000 million.

The statistics available for industrial output are surprisingly inadequate in a number of ways. The only comprehensive figures are given in the UN *Yearbook of Industrial Statistics*, but these apply to different years, many states are omitted altogether, and different criteria are employed. They also demonstrate the distortions inevitable when local values are translated into some international standard, in this case the US dollar. Several East European states have two separate and official dollar conversion rates for their currencies: a 'basic' one, and a non-commercial rate, generally for tourists. The UN statistics have been calculated according to the basic rate, but if these were comparable, the value of manufacturing output in Poland, for example, would have been close to that of West Germany. For the purposes of this map such figures have been converted according to the non-commercial rate.

20. Technological Power

The number of scientists and engineers which each state has in relation to its total population is clearly linked to the size of its manufacturing output — as comparison with *Map 19: Industrial Power* shows. Industrial powers have much greater resources with which to sustain and promote research and development. The inset map, *Brain Drain*, adds the point that there is an international flow of skilled professional and technical labour from the poor states to the rich — labour which is trained at the expense of the poor to benefit the rich.

Given the lacklustre performance in manufacturing output of some East European states, such as Poland and Czechoslovakia, it may seem strange that they should possess so high a proportion of scientists and engineers: as high as Japan and twice as high as West Germany. The answer must lie in their wasteful use of all resources, human as well as material, under the dominion of a distended bureaucracy.

One important aspect of technological power not portrayed on the map is ownership of patents and trademarks. The rich states extend their dominion in technology by either preventing access to certain processes or by exacting a high price for them. Of the patents granted to foreigners in 50 poor states in 1972, no less than 40.6 per cent were owned in the USA, 11.5 per cent in West Germany, 9.6 per cent in Switzerland and 8.9 per cent in the United Kingdom. Of the trademarks registered by foreigners in 54 poor states in 1974, no less than 34.3 per cent were owned in the USA, 15.1 per cent in Japan, 12.2 per cent in the United Kingdom, 9.2 per cent in West Germany and 7 per cent in France. (UNCTAD, *The Role of the Patent System*, 1975 and *The Impact of Trademarks on the Development Process of Developing Countries*, 1977).

21. Dependence and Diversity

This map shows how many states are dependent, for the majority of their export income, on the sale of either one product or a very small number of products. The most extreme case is Oman, where the whole of its export income comes from oil.

The economic weakness of a state dependent upon a single major export is self-evident, especially when it is poor, in competition with other poor states and with the rich as well, and when the product is an agricultural commodity. Not only is there the persistent threat of bad or too bountiful harvests, there is also the threat that access to major traditional markets might be denied: when major customers are also a producer, as with sugar for example, they can take steps to protect their own production at others' expense.

Some poor countries appear to have a stronger, more diversified economic base than they have in reality, since their principal export also takes a partly manufactured form. Bangladesh offers a striking example: 25 per cent of its export income comes from raw jute; but another 25 per cent comes from textile products made mainly from jute and a further 33 per cent comes from woven non-cotton textiles, which are also mainly made of jute. A rare example among rich states is New Zealand: fully two-thirds of New Zealand's exports are animal products.

It should be noted that the statistics do not include tourism nor do they include income from the services offered by tax havens (see *Map 37: The Islands of the Blessed*). For some states, notably in the Caribbean, these are a substantial source of foreign income.

22. Trade Power

This is a graphically distorted map which reveals the extent to which international trade is dominated by a relatively few rich states. In 1978, the whole of Africa emerges as less powerful in trading terms than the

United Kingdom; and the whole of South and Central America as less powerful than the Netherlands.

By comparing this map with *Map 19: Industrial Power* and *Map 23: National Income*, it can be seen that the United States is comparatively weaker in international trade than it is either in manufacturing output, or in the value of its gross national product.

The USSR's relative weakness as a trading power — compared, say, with population (see *Map 3: The State by Population*) with industrial output (see *Map 19: Industrial Power*) or with military power (see *Map 8: Military Spending*) — is also apparent.

As *Map 21: Dependence and Diversity* shows, the weakness of the small trading states is compounded by their dependence on one or two export commodities. Because the poor countries are marginal to international trade, they remain poor; because they are poor, they remain marginal.

The gross national product (GNP) of states in 1977 is shown by a graphic distortion which preserves, as in other maps of this kind, the geographical relationship between states. The annual average rate of growth or decline in GNP per head is shown in colour. (GNP measures a country's total annual income including net earnings from abroad.) What the map underlines is the vast discrepancies between states in both national income and rate of growth.

23. National Income

The most notable increases in the growth rate of GNPs during the seventies have generally been due to one of two factors: either the possession of oil (see *Map 16: Oil Power*); or, participation in the international assembly line of manufacture, where much of the processing has increasingly gone to states able to provide a skilled, controlled, and relatively low-paid labour force, along with tax concessions (see *Map 37: Islands of the Blessed*).

The inset map, *People and Purses*, shows the amount of GNP, or national income, available per head of population. Of course, the greater a state's population, the more it must earn to sustain the well-being of its people.

National income statistics must be viewed with particular caution as pointed out in the Introduction. They do not measure adequately either the value of subsistence production or the value of domestic labour. Further, the measure of national income statistics is the national currency of a single state, the USA, which is vulnerable to movements in foreign exchange rates. To say that the national income of Switzerland, for instance, has increased within a few days by 1 per cent because the Swiss franc has risen in that proportion against the US dollar is manifestly absurd. Yet it is standard practice in national income comparisons.

It is by now well-known that most poor states, generally situated in the southern part of the world, are becoming poorer in relation to the rich, generally situated in the northern part of the world. This map measures the extent of the accumulated debt of poor states, and the degree to which that debt has recently grown or declined. The inset map shows the drain on export income of debt servicing charges and debt repayments.

24. The Debt-Laden South

What the map as a whole shows is the increasing instability of an international economic system in which many states are unable to live within their straitened means, let alone develop their economies — and in which the related fear of debt repudiation and state bankruptcy fuels the further growth of debt. (For manifestations of this increasing instability see *Map 58: Credit Runs Riot* and *Map 59: Panic Stations*.)

In many instances, obligations to foreign creditors can be met only by contracting new debts, thereby increasing the overall burden with its corresponding drain on future income. When creditors are unwilling to provide more loans, as has happened already to both Zaire and Turkey, formal bankruptcy can only be avoided by postponing debt repayments.

An increase in debt does not invariably mean an increase in economic vulnerability. Mexico and Venezuela, for example, have found no difficulty in borrowing huge sums of money in the expectation (shared by their creditors) of future income from oil exports. At the same time, however, the oil price rises that enhance the economic prospects of a Mexico or a Venezuela add correspondingly to the difficulties and costs of other states.

To be sure, among the states affected by the weight of debt are many in the rich northern part of the world. And likewise, such states are driven to increase their external public debt. But the problems of rich industrial states are of a different order from those of the poor states. They are better able to regain a surplus in their balance of payments by increasing exports, especially to the oil exporting states.

25. Margins of Safety

This map shows the size of the gold and foreign currency reserves held by each state in relation to its monthly imports bill: how long each state could sustain its current level of imports without additional earnings from exports.

It must be emphasized that the same figure has a different significance for the rich and for the poor. States whose sources of export income are diverse have much greater flexibility than those dependent on income from one or very few products (see *Map 21: Dependence and Diversity*).

Gold and foreign exchange reserves represent a form of liquid capital to meet deficits in current payments and to repay debt. The gold content of reserves in the map was valued, according to the practice of the World Bank, at the 'official' price of US$ 42.2 per ounce. This is well below the average market price in the recent past. Some governments have accordingly revalued their gold holdings, but while this would make very little difference to the value of reserves held by the poor, it would greatly increase the value of reserves held by the rich — especially the USA, West Germany, France, the Netherlands, Italy and, of course, South Africa.

For reasons best known to themselves, the USSR and states in Eastern Europe do not disclose the value or content of their reserves.

26. Government Income

This graphically distorted map shows each state's share of total world-wide government income from taxes, levies and direct production. The annual average rate of growth or decline of this share is shown in colour.

Gross domestic product (GDP) measures the total wealth generated within a state each year. By comparison with gross national product (GNP), the subject of *Map 23: National Income*, it excludes income payable abroad and excludes income from foreign sources. Reservations on GNP statistics, given in the note to Map 23, apply equally to GDP figures, but additional reservations are needed here. Although the data for most states has been averaged out over a period of three years, 1975–77, for some states three-year comparisons were not available, and for others statistics had to be taken for earlier years. Further, in some cases the figure for a government's share of GDP dates from a different year to that of the GDP figure itself. It is very unlikely though that this invalidates the comparison.

Figures for the USSR and similar states are based differently from those for the rest of the world. We have used those that are closest to UN national income accounting practice.

The wealth of governments, of course, does not necessarily corres-pond to the wealth, let alone the size, of their respective populations. For comparison, see *Map 3: The State by Population* and *Map 23: National Income*.

27. The State Apparatus

This map shows the number of people, as a proportion of total popula-tion, employed by each state for the purpose of internal security.

Some states appear to include in their definition all those who perform police functions of any kind and this must explain the extra-ordinarily high figure for Sweden, for example — 3,655 members of internal security forces for each 100,000 population.

States which include various forms of people's militia or home guard in their statistics are identified on the map. Such forces are used to supplement conventional police. East Germany, for instance, has less than one hundred conventional police for every 100,000 inhabitants, but when the people's militia is included the figure soars to 2,443. Another interesting example is the United States, where a National Guard is used in such circumstances as serious rioting. In the USA, the number of conventional police is 299 per 100,000 population, but when the National Guard are included the figure rises to 515. Both Denmark and Portugal have sizeable 'home guards'. Finally, Switzerland's internal security forces include a large force of reservists which leads to the enormous figure of 7,766 for every 100,000 people. To show how such inclusions may distort the statistics one need only compare with these examples the figure for the United Kingdom of 44.7.

We would have preferred to portray the state apparatus in terms of administrative employment by central and local government, but astonishingly, relevant figures of any kind are available for very few states and when they are, they involve widely different definitions of government employees. In some cases workers in nationalized industries are included, along with teachers and soldiers; in others teachers and soldiers are included, but not workers in nationalized industries; in still others, only those directly involved in government administration are included, even excluding those administering state welfare schemes. As examples of the wide discrepancies in the statistics, official Russian figures for 1978 suggest that some two and a half million out of a total labour force of 109 million (or 2.16 per cent) belong to the apparatus of government, economic and cooperative management and public organizations. While official Danish figures suggest there are some 678,000 public employees out of an economically active population of two and a half million — over 26 per cent.

Such material as is available, and could be made consistent, is shown in the inset map. It includes employees in state health and welfare schemes, but excludes teachers, soldiers and workers in state or para-statal industries.

This map shows the involvement of the military in the government of states, wherever it is substantial, at the end of 1978. The military have not stood still since then, of course. Idi Amin's regime in Uganda was overthrown only for its civilian successor to be displaced by a military coup. Liberia and Surinam both acquired military regimes in 1980 and South Korea, while retaining a civilian government facade, entered the eighties under military command.

A state under martial law is one in which the law governing the armed forces applies to the entire population. A military regime is one in which members of the armed forces compose the principal agency of government. A regime with 'substantial military participation' is one in which the principal agency of government may have a majority of civilians, but crucial positions, including some not directly connected with the armed forces, are held by members of the military. States with 'regimes (as at the end of 1978) established by military coup' have governments which have been essentially continuous since the coup which determined the regime.

Some states, for example Malawi, have civilian or largely civilian dictatorships which are to a greater or lesser degree dependent on military backing. These have not been included since they are not primarily instances of military government.

This map shows the relative importance attached by states to invest-ment in soldiers and investment in teachers. It also shows the number of

28. Military Government

29. Bullets and Blackboards

soldiers employed by each state in relation to its population.

The ratio of soldiers to population gives no indication of the size of individual armies. For such an impression, comparison should be made with *Map 3: The State by Population*. China, for example, may have a low ratio of soldiers to population, but so large is its population that it has more soldiers than any other state. Nor does a low ratio of soldiers to population necessarily denote a relatively libertarian regime or a relatively contented populace. The sustenance of oppression or the control of discontent often call on the employment not of soldiers but of special methods (see *Map 31: Scourges of the State*) and special agents (see *Map 27: The State Apparatus*).

Particular events may radically alter or at least temporarily distort information on individual states. For example, the overthrow of the fascist regime in Portugal ended a system of military conscription, for warfare abroad, which had made Portugal's ratio of soldiers to population among the highest in the world. And since 1974, the changing situation in South-East Asia produced first a large reduction and then a large increase in the relative sizes of the armies in the area.

30. Conscription and Conscience

This map shows the extent of compulsory military service for men in the mid seventies and the status of conscientious objection in the early seventies. In some states, military service is compulsory but selective and the colour for these has been cross-hatched with the colour for the appropriate period of service. Reserve duty is also shown.

In some states, for example Poland and the Netherlands, the length of compulsory service in the army differs from that in other branches of the armed forces. In such cases, it is the length of army service which has been taken as the standard. In other states, notably Sweden and Portugal, a flexible period of military service applies and here the shorter has been used.

In Israel and Burma conscription applies to women as well as men. There are signs that other states may adopt this practice. In some cases conscription applies to only a section of the population: in South Africa, only to whites; in Cyprus, only to Greeks; in Israel only to Jews and Druzes.

No state accepts political opinion as sufficient grounds for release from military service: conscientious objection is essentially regarded by states as a concession to be restricted as far as possible rather than as a right to be enjoyed. In many, even religious grounds are so circumscribed that only members of a particular sect qualify — for example, the Mennonites in Mexico, Bolivia and Paraguay.

31. Scourges of the State

A healthy society, Plato believed, would have no use for doctors or lawyers. By analogy, it may be argued that a world without states would have no need for the prisons, the torture chambers and the places of execution that this map records.

States rarely acknowledge the application of torture or the existence of political prisoners and in the reporting of these the work of Amnesty International is crucial. For this reason, though, it is important to emphasize that the absence of individual symbols on this map may only mean that there have been no reported instances in the years covered.

The law on the death penalty is sometimes misleading for a number of reasons. In the United Kingdom, for example, the death penalty remains on the statute book but for use only in cases of treason and certain forms of piracy. It has not been imposed since 1964 and is popularly believed to have been abolished altogether. The fact that it remains on the statute book, however, means that it may be much more readily reinstated. In other states, for example Australia and the USA, the death penalty comes within the jurisdiction of constituent states rather than the federal government. In both cases, some state governments have abolished the death penalty while others have retained it.

The number of prisoners in relation to total population is shown in colour. Some of the statistics are confusingly low and may well denote the very opposite of the contented, peaceful conditions they appear to indicate. In Amin's Uganda and Pol Pot's Kampuchea, for example, there were less protracted ways of dealing with opponents than confining them in jails.

32. Refugees

The world refugee population is large, fluctuating and poorly recorded. This map shows the numbers of new refugees between 1972 and 1979. Such refugees may either have been displaced within their own state or have been obliged to move to others across state frontiers.

Major refugee movements both before and since this period have not been included. For example, the Nigerian civil war over Biafra in 1967–1970 led to a major internal displacement of population; substantial flows of refugees have moved from Cuba to the USA both before and after the period; and since 1979 there have been regular reports of large numbers leaving Afghanistan and various provincial states in north-east India. A single exception has been made. The Palestinians have been included because of their continuing political importance and because, unlike so many other refugees, they have scarcely been resettled or absorbed.

33. Languages of Rule

A language of rule is one which is used by a political and/or economic elite to reinforce its control and sustain its cohesion. It effectively helps to deny participation in government or administration by those who do not speak it. It promotes, most notably in Africa, a closer association between the elites of individual states than with their own populations.

The map identifies the varying status of languages imported or created by such elites. It shows where such languages are official, where they are not official but widely used in government and business, and where they merely have status as old imperial languages. It also shows where popular, creole forms of old imperial languages have developed, particularly in the Caribbean, and where the majority of the poor are unable to speak the official language, as is the case with poor, indigenous Indian populations in parts of South America.

Where languages of rule have been imported their status as official languages may be temporary, as proved the case in Morocco (French) or as may happen throughout Malaysia (English), where in 1980, only Sarawak maintains English as an official language. In some countries – Ireland, the Lebanon and Tanzania – there are two or more official languages, only one of which is the language of the majority. This is shown by cross-hatching colours and adding symbols for the minority language or languages.

Greenland does not appear on this map but as a province of Denmark, Danish is its official language, while the majority of its population of 48,000 speak an Eskimo language.

The map is a contemporary rather than historical record. Portuguese, for example, was brought by conquest to what is now called Brazil. It then so far displaced the indigenous languages as to no longer constitute a language of rule.

34. Religions of Rule

The belief in future fulfilment, prosperity and security; the representation of that belief in ritual; its supporting justification by reference to holy writ, interpreted by a special category of people; and its accommodation within state-supported or state-associated institutions: such are the hallmarks of many religions. In this sense, official Marxism-Leninism is such a religion: with its concentration on the benefits of the future from the sacrifices of the present; its conventional parades and ceremonies; its revealed truths, whose texts are to be interpreted only by those appointed to do so; and its association with the power of the state. Furthermore, like some other religions, it has its own schismatic orthodoxies (the Moscow and the Peking denominations); its populist low church heterodoxies (Titoism in Yugoslavia); its anathematized heresy (Trotskyism); and its fundamentalist sects (revolutionary Marxism).

A religion of rule is defined as one which is professed by the governing classes and which sustains their solidarity. Poland provides a good example of the first case, since official Marxism-Leninism, of the Moscow denomination, rules over a population almost entirely Roman Catholic in allegiance. An example of the second case is the United Kingdom. Here the majority of the population is either secular or holds a variety of religious beliefs. But the Church of England is the official state religion, its bishops are automatically members of the upper house of parliament and it retains control through its official status.

In dealing with Christianity, Catholicism and Protestantism are distinguished only where one of these is clearly dominant, and no distinction is made between different versions of Protestantism. As far as Islam is concerned, the only distinction made is between Sunni and Shia, such variants as do exist being accommodated within each dominant strain.

Sites of recent religious conflict are shown on the map, but only where there is current violence on religious grounds, or where there is a significant religious component. In Kampuchea, this reflects the struggle between Peking- and Moscow-backed forces; in Afghanistan, between Islam and Moscow.

35. The Public and the Private

These two maps *Big Money* and *Big Business*, are intended to show the wealth, and therefore power, of some of the world's major banks and some of the largest transnationals compared with many independent states.

Big Money shows the gold and foreign currency reserves of individual states in relation to the assets of banks in the private sector (that is, not central banks). While it is normal for a bank's assets to be almost entirely equalled by its liabilities, it is almost always true that a state's national reserves are more than matched by its foreign debts.

Since the map was prepared, the Crédit Agricole de France replaced the Bank of America as the world's largest bank, with assets of US$105,000 million. Yet in 1976, no state had assets larger than the Bank of America and only one, West Germany, had assets above those of the National Westminster Bank, then only the twentieth in size. At the same time, although the Cantonal Bank of St Gall, in Switzerland, was the world's 300th bank in size, many states, especially in South America and Africa, had reserves lower than its assets.

The reserve figures for the United Kingdom are now considerably higher for a number of reasons: partly because the British government has pursued a tighter monetary policy with related high interest rates, and partly because North Sea oil and oil price rises have produced a strong currency and an enormous inflow of funds.

As with *Map 25: Margins of Safety*, it has been impossible to compare the national reserves of the USSR and associated states because they are not declared.

Big Business compares the gross national product of individual states with the sales income of a range of US transnationals, or multinationals, in 1977. While a corporation's turnover is not the precise equivalent of a state's GNP, the two are close enough for useful comparison. Both Guyana and Surinam, together with many states in Africa, had GNPs lower than the sales income of the US owned company, Time Inc.

36. The Nationality of Transnationals

This map demonstrates the dichotomy in the nature of transnational enterprise. While their name and their method of functioning would suggest allegiance to no particular state interests, they remain tied to the state where they are officially based. The pressures of world-wide competition lead transnational companies to cross state boundaries. The drive for power and the need for support from the state means that their 'nationality' should never be overlooked.

The map confirms common knowledge, that the majority of transnationals are owned in the states of Western Europe and, in particular, the United States, home base of the largest transnationals in the world.

37. The Islands of the Blessed

This map shows some of the many ways in which corporations and business generally seek to avoid state taxation. It also shows how many states, especially islands in the Atlantic and the Pacific, find legal means of benefiting from this search. To emphasize the role of islands, all the states involved have been artificially depicted as such.

The map isolates tax havens, flags of convenience, free production zones and offshore manufacturing zones as the primary means of tax avoidance. It is in the nature of the topic that such a map cannot be exhaustive; private capital's search for havens of one sort or another is relentless, inventive, and often successfully cloaked in secrecy.

The difference between major and minor tax havens is one of financial importance, as judged by the private banking sources consulted.

States offering registration of flags of convenience are those which provide shipping companies with the advantages of nominal or low taxation, and little or no regulation of safety or working conditions on board.

Free production zones are areas set aside for offshore manufacturing or assembly plants. Major zones are defined as those in which 10,000 or more workers were employed in 1975. Offshore plants may operate both inside and outside free production zones. They are based on local labour but export all their output. They enjoy tax and customs privileges. The free production zones featured on this map relate to Africa, Asia and Latin America only. Others, in Ireland and, increasingly Eastern Europe, have been excluded on the grounds that they are as yet unimportant in their economic and social effect on their host economies.

38. The Flight to Work

This map shows the numbers of people prepared to go abroad in search of work, their states of origin and the states to which they are drawn.

While international agencies such as the United Nations and the International Labour Office in Geneva are permanently working to compile and publish statistics on population movements and employment, there is no single world-wide study of people seeking work across national frontiers. As a result this map has been produced in the full knowledge that it is incomplete, dependent as it is on occasional regional statistics and personal estimates of individuals. Some states, such as Australia, Venezuela and north-east India, are known to attract immigrant workers, but no figures or estimates were available.

One of the difficulties is that in some cases most of the people who enter a state in search of work do so illegally. This is particularly true of the United States where most illegal entrants do so from Mexico and most of these, perhaps two-thirds of the total, are Mexican citizens. Estimates of the illegal migrant population 'range from two to twelve million' according to a *White House Fact Sheet*, 4 August 1977. The figure on this map of three million migrant workers in the US is an estimate prepared by Roger Böhning of the ILO.

Migrant labour is a major source of income to both the families left behind and their states of origin. At the end of 1973, West Germany was paying children's allowances for some 850,000 children who were living abroad and who had at least one parent working in West Germany. These were going to the following:

Turkey	515,200
Yugoslavia	148,100
Italy	80,900
Spain	42,500
Portugal	32,600
Greece	28,700

The number of foreign children who were resident in West Germany and receiving payments at the same time came to 154,400. (UN, *The Welfare of Migrant Workers and Their Families*, Report of a seminar in Yugoslavia, New York 1976.)

A further example of the value of migrant labour to their states of origin relates to African migrant workers in France. In 1973, transfers from migrant workers in France contributed 24.7 per cent of Morocco's total revenue from external sources, 20 per cent of Algeria's and 11.6 per cent of Tunisia's. (Roberto Aliboni ed., *Arab Industrialization and Economic Integration*, London, Croom Helm 1979.)

39. Exploitation

Ideally, a measure of exploitation would compare the output of all productive workers (i.e. workers whose labour results in essential ingredients for further production) with their income. Such a measure does not exist, since productive and unproductive workers are not differentiated analytically or statistically; since inessential is not differentiated from essential output; since statistics do not cover all economic activity, but only part of it; and since they are not truly international in their scope.

So instead of using a formula such as: value added in productive activity divided by wages in cash and kind for productive activity, we have had to settle for the following: value of gross output in manufacturing, less wages and salaries in manufacturing, divided by wages and salaries in manufacturing.

The results of applying the latter formula were divided into five levels of exploitation: first level — below 4; second level — 4 to 6.99; third level — 7 to 9.99; fourth level — 10 to 12.99; and fifth level — over 12.

The data itself presented certain problems. Some governments report the value of gross output at factor cost, the cost to the producer of the elements of production excluding indirect taxes but including subsidies; some, at producers' prices, including indirect taxes, but excluding subsidies; and some adopt hybrid definitions. Some governments make an attempt to quantify non-wage payments, most do not. In some states — the richer ones — salaries form a large component of the labour bill, in most they do not. In some states, manufacturing covers a far wider range of economic activity than in others. In most but not all cases, a three-year average was used, in others, the three most recent years available, and occasionally, less than three years.

Overall, it must be admitted, we believe that the available data gives a biased picture. Exploitation in rich states appears to be lower than exploitation in poor states, when the opposite may well be the case. It is to be hoped that this first world map of exploitation may lead to a more refined study.

40. The Labour Force

These two maps describe the nature of the labour force in individual states: *Workers on the Land* and *Workers in Industry*. Neither includes the service sector which, everywhere, although for very different reasons, is both large and growing.

Both maps confirm the dependence of poor states on agricultural labour and production. But some poor states, for example Zambia and Uganda, show a surprisingly small percentage of their population to be working in agriculture, together with an equally, and not surprising, small percentage working in industry. This is because in many poor states, much of what is termed 'economically active population' is actually unemployed or is engaged on the fringes of the economy in a multitude of subsistence 'service' capacities. Although this would appear to be a subject on which there would be fairly reliable and complete statistics, this is far from the case. Many African states clearly have great difficulty in establishing the nature of their workforces and may even be reluctant to reveal information.

Figures for China, which are not otherwise available, have been taken from estimates provided by Jon Sigurdson, in *Rural Industrialization in China*, Harvard 1977.

This map shows the percentage of women workers in the non-domestic labour force and gives an index of the degree of sexual discrimination in jobs.

In many states whose workforce is employed primarily in agriculture (see *Map 40: The Labour Force*), women workers inhabit a twilight zone between agricultural and domestic labour. This often leads to strange statistical conclusions such as the apparently low percentage of women workers in both Equatorial Guinea and Guinea-Bissau, and where the actual numbers are known to be high. By comparison, it would be expected that the number of women workers in Islamic states would be low and this is borne out by the map.

The index of sexual discrimination in jobs is based on the proportion of women (or men) who would have to change their occupational or industrial classification for there to be sex equality in employment. Inevitably, the definition of inequality involves an important component of status and this must reflect in some way the personal judgement of its source, Elise Boulding *et al., Handbook of International Data on Women,* 1976. Yet the ranking confirms general knowledge: that women enjoy greater job equality in Eastern Europe than in Western Europe and that there is most discrimination in the Islamic states of the Middle East.

There is one major reservation to be made. Absence of discrimination in dangerous or debilitatingly heavy manual labour is not necessarily a sign of equality. In many Asian states, women act as unskilled assistants to more skilled male workers.

41. Women Workers

In this map we have attempted to peer behind the single concept of trade unionism to the widely differing realities of trade union freedom and confinement. In some states, trade unions are more or less independent bodies, able to take most decisions related to their interests without interference from the state, except in times of national emergency. In most states, whatever the official pretensions, independent trade unionism does not exist.

As far as we are aware, no such map has previously been attempted. The categories and definitions were determined on the advice of leading international trade union officials. Although the first two categories divide states into those where independent trade unions comprise more than and less than half the labour force, it was not our intention to quantify in detail the numbers of workers in trade unions. In fact, in the United Kingdom for instance, almost half of all employed workers are in unions and the trend is upwards. In the United States, for comparison, only about a quarter of the workforce is unionized and the proportion is declining.

Trade unions that are totally controlled, as in the USSR, Eastern Europe and a number of Asian and African states, are essentially organs of government with no independence of decision. Trade unions that are tightly controlled, as in many other African states, have independence of decision in form, but are in fact permitted such independence only when there is no conflict with major government policies.

There was some disagreement between trade union experts on the appropriate category for trade unionism in certain African states, such as Zambia, Nigeria, Ghana and Kenya and also others in Latin America.

42. The Force of Labour

This map compares the incomes of the top 5 per cent in individual states, with the bottom 20 per cent. Although the statistics used relate to the sixties and the early seventies, no later information was available.

The disparity is large, but in reality may be even greater. For a number of reasons, the incomes of the rich are systematically understated by the statistics. It is now widely recognized that the rich enjoy various forms of consumption outside the expenditure of their official after-tax incomes. In Western capitalist societies and their imitators elsewhere, executives, for instance, are provided with forms of untaxed income in kind: the use of company-owned apartments, cars and even

43. Rich and Poor People

planes; participation in company-subsidized schemes for private medical treatment and the private education of children; and a whole multitude of minor benefits which can be broadly described as expense-account entertainment. In addition, instead of salary increases which bring with them a high rate of tax, they are frequently offered option and other equity allowances likely to produce a capital gain and be taxed at a much lower rate, if at all.

Although figures are not available for incomes in the USSR and Eastern Europe, bureaucrats there also have access to privileged consumption beyond their official incomes: through state-supplied living quarters and transport, special medical facilities, special schools or places at schools, and their own shops which make available rare or subsidized goods.

The inset map shows the dramatic division between rich and poor within groups of economies determined by its source, UNCTAD, and which includes Yugoslavia among the 'developed market economies' and Cuba among the 'developed centrally planned' ones.

44. Our Daily Bread

This map shows the number of calories available per head of population in each state and the incidence of famines between 1950 and 1979.

The minimum calorie intake, as defined by the World Health Organization, takes into account climatic conditions, types of work, sex and average weight, and has been incorporated into the figures on which this map is based.

The most extreme cases of states with mass calorie deprivation correspond with the Sahel region of West Africa which suffered severe drought and famine between 1972 and 1974 and which reached their peak in 1973. The Sahel drought is illustrated in the inset map.

Although some rich states, such as Canada, West Germany and Sweden, appear to be less privileged than the USSR and Czechoslovakia, it should be remembered that calorie intake is the most simple of food measures. The diet of the former may involve a higher intake of protein, vitamins and other food values.

The following table provides comparative information on protein deficiency. It appeared in the Food and Agricultural Organization's *Fourth World Survey*, 1977.

state	year of survey	age group (in years)	% suffering from protein energy malnutrition		
			Severe	Moderate	Total
India		1–5	2.0	52.7	54.7
Rwanda	1971	0–5	9.8	44.9	54.7
Cameroon	1973	0–5	4.4	36.4	40.8
Cen. Af. Rep.	1972	0–5	3.0	36.4	39.4
Guatemala	1967	0–4	5.9	26.5	32.4
Guyana	1971	0–4	1.3	30.8	32.1
Haiti	1971	0–5	6.0	25.0	31.0
Burundi	1972	0–5	2.2	28.7	30.4
El Salvador	1967	0–4	3.1	22.9	26.0
Kenya	1968		1.0	25.0	26.0
Brazil	1970	0–4	6.3	18.9	25.2
Colombia	1968		1.7	19.3	21.0
Jamaica	1970	0–3	1.4	18.0	19.4
Barbados	1969	0–4	1.2	15.3	16.5
Venezuela	1971	1–6	0.9	14.5	15.4

For Barbados, El Salvador, Guatemala, Guyana, Jamaica and Venezuela, these were national samples; for Cameroon, the sample was limited to Douala; for the remainder, no further details are given.

Protein deficiency is permanently damaging to small children since it affects the development of the brain.

During the Sahel famine 1972–74, whole populations were uprooted and people died in hundreds of thousands. Exceptionally low rainfall had aggravated the cumulative effects of unrestrained grazing, excessive cultivation and short-sighted social policies.

Early reports suggest that the current famine (1980) in East Africa, the result of civil conflict and war, as well as agricultural neglect and inadequate rainfall, may claim even more victims.

Susan George, citing a National Geographic magazine report of a satellite photograph of the Sahel region, provides a useful correction to the 'climatic' explanation for the tragedy. The photograph shows 'a hexagonal island of green in the tan sea of the Sahel. Inspection revealed it to be a quarter-million acre modern ranch, fenced off with barbed-wire from the surrounding desert. Inside, other fences divide the ranch into five sectors, with cattle grazing a single sector at a time. Though the ranch has been in operation only seven years, the rotational grazing has made the difference between pasture and desert. (Susan George, *How the Other Half Dies: The Real Reasons for World Hunger*, Penguin 1976, page 45.)

45. Bill of Health

This map shows infant mortality rates, life expectancy figures for both men and women and also the number of hospital beds in proportion to population.

Infant mortality is the single most important factor in the measurement of life expectancy at birth and a high rate of infant mortality will reduce significantly figures for life expectancy.

Incidence of hospital beds as an index of medical provision should not be taken to imply a judgement on the value of Western allopathic medicine compared with traditional homeopathic systems. There is no means of telling the extent of provision of traditional systems of medicine, and therefore no way of using them for international comparison; and Western medicine is internationally dominant.

46. The Right to Learn

This map shows the extent of illiteracy in individual states. It also shows the percentage enrolment of the population of appropriate age in primary, secondary and tertiary education. In some states, children of secondary school age are still at primary schools, thus inflating the percentage in primary education and reducing the percentage in secondary education. In Gabon, the Lebanon and Hong Kong for example, this pushes the primary school figure to above 100 per cent.

The limited resources that poor states are able to devote to higher education are in many cases ultimately diverted abroad (see *Map 20: Technological Power* and *Map 38: The Flight to Work*), or into the service of local subsidiaries of transnational corporations whose profits are exported (see *Map 36: The Nationality of Transnationals*). What remains is often the more irrelevant for being too closely modelled on imported curricula which reflect the needs and conditions of alien societies. The predictable result is a high drop-out rate and the explosive resentment that go with it.

47. The Longer Reach

There are few ways in which the citizen can reach out from immediate circumstances to give and receive news, ideas and opinions, in exchanges which constitute the vital source of intellectual emancipation and which so many governments see as a challenge and even a threat. The two such instruments chosen are the telephone, an essentially private form of communication, and newsprint, essentially a means of public communication.

It is certainly true that in many societies poverty is principally responsible for the lack of both. But, as the map reveals, there are some states, the Soviet Union for example, where neither economic backwardness nor widespread illiteracy can explain the relatively small number of telephones available or the relatively low consumption of newsprint.

Of course, newsprint consumption levels can give no indication of who owns or controls the press, or show degrees of press freedom. Nor does access to a telephone guarantee private and free communication.

48. Holes in the Safety Net

This map shows the percentage of welfare payments made by states to individuals, as a percentage of gross domestic product. The data for the map have been taken from the eighth and ninth international inquiries into *The Cost of Social Security*, conducted by the International Labour Office and covering the years 1971–74 in the eighth inquiry and 1976–1979 in the ninth inquiry. Most data comes from the ninth inquiry, except in the case of fourteen states.

A comparison of the results of the two inquiries confirms the truth of that most uncharitable of injunctions 'to those who have, let more be given'. Where comparison between 1971 and 1974 was possible, the proportion of net welfare receipts to gross domestic product fell in every state in Africa, every state in Asia apart from Japan; and every state in South America, except for oil-rich Venezuela. The proportion rose only in Oceania, and throughout Europe except for Czechoslovakia and Greece.

49. The Swelling Cities

This map deals with the internal migration of people. It shows that in most states there is a persistent net migration of country dwellers to towns and cities. Since the total populations of all states except East Germany have increased (see *Map 3: The State by Population*) this has usually been accompanied by a less significant rise in rural population. In East Germany both urban and rural populations have declined, partly as a result of large-scale migration to West Germany in the period before the Berlin Wall was built. In Western and Eastern Europe and North America there has been an actual decline in rural population and this is shown on the map.

A UN monitoring report, *World Population Trends and policies 1977*, 1979, has compared the attitudes of various governments towards population distribution between cities and countryside and the policies pursued.

Out of the 146 governments surveyed, 112 regarded the rate of urbanization as either 'substantially unacceptable' or 'extremely unacceptable'. Yet only 80 of these claim to have policies directed at decelerating – not reversing – the process and 16 had policies of no intervention whatsoever.

The survey produced some strange anomalies. Bhutan and Cyprus regarded their spatial distribution as 'slightly unacceptable', Brazil and Saudi Arabia as 'substantially unacceptable', yet all four were pursuing policies of 'acceleration' of urban growth. On the other hand, East Germany, Hungary, Czechoslovakia and Sweden regarded their spatial distribution as 'entirely acceptable', while at the same time they were pursuing attempts to decelerate the process.

50. Slumland

This map uses access to safe water supplies as the most unambiguous index available of urban health. Other indices, such as area of floor space per person or the number of people per room or dwelling unit are clearly open to misinterpretation when compared internationally.

The map also shows percentage areas of slums in many of the world's major cities. Since the source of information was the United Nations *Second World Housing Survey*, 1974, the most recent available, and only selected cities were included, there appear to be obvious omissions: perhaps Kingston (Jamaica), Port of Spain (Trinidad), La Paz (Bolivia), Jakarta (Indonesia) and Soweto (South Africa) – to name but a few examples. And since economic growth rates are now declining almost everywhere, and the proportion of slum dwellers in the urban population was increasing even in the period of high economic growth, it is reasonable to assume that the situation today is substantially worse than is conveyed by the map.

This map deals with criminal activity as defined by state authorities and also with murder as the supreme human crime. Definitions of crime are obviously open to varieties of interpretation by individual states but in general all crimes which come to the attention of the police, other than traffic offences, are included. Murder is defined as any act performed (successfully) with the intention of taking human life. This definition excludes manslaughter and abortion, but not infanticide.

The fact that statistics can be very misleading is exemplified by definitions of crime in South Africa. There are serious crimes in South Africa which would not be regarded as crimes at all by other states, notably sexual relations between members of different races as defined by South Africa's Immorality Act. Figures for murder, while high, are in reality much higher still, since murders within the black community are sometimes not brought to the attention of the police. And although the numbers may be numerically marginal, statistics for murder do not include those who have died under police interrogation from allegedly natural causes. The peculiarly high figure for murder in the Lebanon may be explained by the escalating political violence that preceded the civil war.

The principal source of statistics used for this map, the International Criminal Police Organization (Interpol) offers some words of caution:

'The General Secretariat simply reproduces the information given on the forms from each country . . . The information . . . is unsophisticated but uniform . . .

'We emphasize the fact that the data given in this report is [sic] in no way intended to be used as a basis for comparison between different countries. Our statistics cannot take account of the differences which exist between the definitions of what constitutes an indictable offence in the various national legislatures considered, of the different methods of calculation, nor of any changes in legal definitions, the structure of the various services engaged in criminal investigation and the conditions under which it is carried out, which may have occurred during the period covered by the report. Bearing in mind all these unknown factors, together with others which influence police investigation, the figures which appear in this report must be considered approximate and should therefore be interpreted with great caution.'

51. Law and Disorder

We felt compelled to abandon our original plan for a map on recent rates of unemployment throughout the world for reasons explained in the Introduction.

This chart is taken from one produced by the International Labour Office in 1974. It uses current UN population projections and a rule-of-thumb correlation between total population and economically active population, to present the likely profile of unemployment in rich and poor states up to the year 2150.

Such projections are frequently subject to sudden amendment or refinement which may be caused by new evidence or even new theories. And the chart itself is clearly based on economic trends in the past that may well not be reflected in the future. The difficulties and instabilities of the present world economic system (see Maps 55–59 in particular) point to a period of much slower economic growth than has been known since the second world war, if not to a period of stagnation or even contraction. Such a period, if significantly prolonged, would significantly reduce the economically active proportion to the whole.

At the very least, this chart warns of the blighted future that could affect many millions of lives.

52. The Unemployment Time Bomb

Given the reluctance of the world's states to acknowledge the damage being done to its most basic resources, this map can evoke only some of the worst known examples of pollution to air and sea.

Sea pollution is a phenomenon more recognized than measured. Therefore the map, though based on the data available, remains essen-

53. Fouling the Nest

tially impressionistic and concentrates on those areas known to be most heavily affected.

In the Mediterranean, the problem has reached emergency dimensions and more detailed information is available which is shown in the inset map. But in addition to the pollutants included, there are at least two other major industrial sources of pollution in the Mediterranean: mercury waste and pesticides.

Air pollution is shown by two limited regional studies of the most commonly dangerous industrial pollutants: sulphur dioxide, which becomes sulphuric acid when combined with water vapour and which is a prime cause of chronic lung disease; and lead, which can seriously and permanently damage the nervous system and is particularly dangerous for children.

It is important to emphasize that pollution is neither local nor isolated. For this reason individual, though dramatic, instances of pollution disasters, such as the mercury poisoning at Minimata (Japan), first officially identified in 1956, and the dioxin poisoning in Seveso (Italy) in 1976 have not been included.

54. The Dying Earth

The purpose of this map is to demonstrate not only the steady increase in desert across the earth, but also the part played in this increase by neglect and deliberate injury.

The map identifies bioclimatic zones, shows areas where there is very high or moderate risk of intensifying or extending aridity and some of the major causes. Vulnerable land includes stony or rocky surfaces, areas subject to soil stripping and gully erosion, areas subject to sand movement, and land with excess salt or bad soil structure. Human and animal pressure refers to density of human population and livestock. Human pressure also includes intense pressure of cultivation associated with mechanization.

It has taken thousands of years for large tracts of desert and semi-desert land to develop out of what were once fertile regions: years in which haphazard human encroachment has upset the delicate balance on which ecological renewal depends.

In recent years this encroachment has become more violent. In large parts of Africa for example, population pressure, patterns of land ownership and war have intensified the destruction of land, increased blight to a virtually endemic condition and produced almost permanent famine (see *Map 44: Our Daily Bread*).

Technology has made possible more deliberate large-scale encroachment and drastic changes in land use can be effected. Vast tracts of rain forest in Brazil are now being turned into grazing land, creating a potential desert of the future.

The extension of desert and arid zones has more than local and regional significance. Large-scale changes in land patterns and use can have major effects on both the weather and the renewal of the world's oxygen supply.

In times of war, even more powerful techniques of destruction are employed, and employed deliberately. The inset map shows the extent of war pollution in Vietnam, Kampuchea and Laos. Whole regions have been poisoned and destroyed through the spraying of herbicides and defoliants and bombardment with shrapnel.

The report of the UN Conference on Desertification 1977, concluded that although more than one-third of the earth's land is already arid, declining fertility and productivity, caused by current levels of intensification, will affect the livelihood of well over 600 million people, most of whom live in poor states.

55. Industrial Droop

This map introduces a section on the emerging symptoms of crisis within the world economic system. What it shows specifically is the decline in the growth rates of industrial production between the sixties and the seventies — a decline which continues to accelerate.

The causes are both complex and arguable. The consequences are momentous (see, for example, *Map 56: The First Inflationary Crest, 1974; Map 59: Panic Stations* and *Map 65: Urban Heavings in the Seventies*).

56. The First Inflationary Crest, 1974

There is no more effective form of undermining the social order than through the unexpected and apparently remedyless inequities induced by a high and rising cost of inflation. In so far as there is a single dominant symptom of crisis in the world system, it is precisely this problem of inflation, which governments freely acknowledge but are patently unable to solve.

A huge rise in the price of oil was made by OPEC in September 1973. But this was itself in large measure a response to the surge of inflation from the end of the sixties. By 1971, world inflation was running at an annual 6.6 per cent, and by 1973 at an annual 9.5 per cent. In 1974, it reached 15.1 per cent overall. In some states, notably the United Kingdom, inflation did not crest until 1975, but in the majority of states, inflation had done so in the previous year.

Figures for inflation are not provided by the Soviet Union or states in Eastern Europe. But if the rates of inflation there were, as claimed, lower than in the industrial West, this was at least in part because consumer queues were appreciably longer.

That the world inflationary crisis in 1974 was no isolated phenomenon is already evident. There was a further inflationary surge in the late seventies, a surge that had not yet crested at the start of 1980. At the end of 1979, inflation figures in many states, notably in such major industrial ones as the USA, Canada and the United Kingdom, were already running above the rate in 1974.

57. Funny Money

Whatever the causes of inflation, there can be no doubt that significant among them is a substantial rise in the supply of money, unmatched by a rise in the production of goods and services.

This map shows the growth in the money supply in individual states over a ten-year period, 1968–77. The figures for a few states do not cover the full ten years, because the statistical series of which they were a part changed their bases during the period. Figures for the United States, the dominant state in the world monetary system, appear peculiarly low. But alongside this low increase in the domestic supply of dollars, there was a massive increase in the supply of expatriate dollars, primarily located in what is known as the Euro-dollar market (see *Map 58: Credit Runs Riot*).

The inset map shows how far the purchasing power of the major currencies was eroded between 1950 and 1975.

58. Credit Runs Riot

If inflation is one symptom of increasing economic instability (see *Map 56: The First Inflationary Crest, 1974*) another is the enormous and accelerating growth of credit. The trend to economic crisis is intensified when such credit rises are accompanied by levels of industrial production and gross national product which are in retreat (see *Map 55: Industrial Droop* and *Map 23: National Income*).

Almost all states and international agencies have participated in the scramble for credit. But while some have been able to borrow on the basis of their conspicuous ability to repay (OPEC member states), others (non-OPEC 'developing' states) have been given further credit because of their very inability to meet current obligations.

Most have been accommodated on the Euro-currency market, the fastest growing international credit market and the one least subject to state surveillance and controls. This map shows recent expansion in Euro-currency bank credits which is measured by the foreign currency liabilities of banks in major European states and in the Bahamas, Cayman

Islands, Bahrain, Panama, Japan, Canada, Hong Kong and Singapore.

The Euro-currency market is essentially the market in money held outside its state of origin. About 75 per cent of this market is in expatriate US dollars and the growth in this element has been some ten times the growth in the US domestic money supply during the seventies. This enormous increase in the Euro-dollar sector, with an average annual rate of around 70 per cent in the last decade, has been a primary cause of international credit growth and inflation.

The high and rising cost of credit is shown in the inset map. This is measured as the 'prime rate', or rate of interest charged to best customers, of commercial banks. It is a product of inflation and also a contributory cause, since it often makes borrowing for investment purposes prohibitively expensive and contracts the base of industrial production (see *Map 55: Industrial Droop*).

59. Panic Stations

As a result of the problems depicted in Maps 55–58, there has been an increasing flight from the paper currencies into gold.

The main map shows some of the different features of the gold market: it shows gold producers and levels of gold production; it shows gold holdings of individual states and identified private hoarding; it shows the extent of gold bullion movements throughout the world; and in a graph it shows the annual average increase in the free market price of gold since 1968.

The map indicates the central role played by Switzerland in the world gold market. It is a role essentially supported by special arrangements between leading Swiss banks and the South African Reserve Bank, arrangements which did much to reduce the importance of London, once the centre of the international gold market.

Figures for the Soviet Union's gold production and gold holdings are not made public; but gold production is generally estimated at almost 13 million ounces and holdings have been reported to be over 63 million ounces.

In March 1978, the gold holdings of states within the European Monetary System dropped by almost 20 per cent when corresponding contributions were made to its central pool. Private hoarding is almost invariably secret. We have included estimates by Consolidated Gold Fields for the principal private hoards known to exist in France and India. We have added a Bundesbank estimate for accumulated purchases of Krugerrands (South African gold coins weighing one ounce) in West Germany.

In the United States, it became legal for private citizens to hold and deal in gold at the end of 1974, and this has become a major factor in the international gold market. An even more direct and substantial impact has been made by the New York and Chicago markets in gold futures – contracts to buy or sell specified amounts of gold for a certain price and at a certain date.

Net sales from official monetary gold stocks to private purchasers have consisted in recent years almost entirely of sales from the International Monetary Fund and from the US Treasury. Such sales, at 11.67 million ounces, do not necessarily all find their way into private stocks, since some may have been additions to the gold holdings of certain central banks.

The inset map shows how the flight into gold has been accompanied by a similar movement from the weaker to the stronger currencies.

60. Nuclear Power, No Thanks

By the year 2000, it has been estimated, there will be more than a hundred nuclear power plants which are no longer operational. In addition, there will be hundreds of smaller nuclear installations – research accelerators, fuel enrichment and reprocessing plants, naval reactors, nuclear medical facilities – whose productive lives are at an end. All of them will remain radioactive for hundreds or even thousands of years: an ever-present danger to future generations.

Opposition to nuclear power has taken various forms. In Japan and Yugoslavia, for instance, it is done primarily by law-suit. In some states it has merged into the wider political process. In Sweden, during 1976, it was material in bringing more than four decades of social democratic government to an end. And elsewhere, too, the ballot box has been used to notable effect. In Austria, Denmark, parts of Belgium and parts of the United States, the encroachment of nuclear power has been arrested or slowed by referendum. In other states such as the Soviet Union and Eastern Europe, it is part of a political debate conducted behind closed doors.

The public opposition shown in this map encompasses direct action protests against the whole nuclear energy industry: from uranium mining to the trade in reactors and methods of disposal of nuclear waste. Direct action is shown in all its forms: from industrial strikes and sabotage, demonstrations and festivals, to confrontation and battles with the police. If anything, the extent of such activity is likely to be understated: major West European and American newspapers, which are the source of information for the map, may not have reported many protests which were either small, spontaneous or hidden by authority.

What the map cannot show is the international character of the protest movement: the contingents of Danish protesters in Germany and Sweden; of Germans in France and Switzerland; of French in Germany; of British in France — a character that is a recognition of the degree to which a nuclear facility in one state can affect the environment in another.

Where action has been widespread, as on the Hiroshima–Nagasaki commemoration days of August 1977 in the United States, or the rail transport strike of May 1976 in Australia, symbols have been sited in the appropriate national or regional capital city.

While we had intended to indicate all sites of nuclear accidents grave enough to lead to a shutdown of a nuclear facility, there were so few plants *not* affected that the map would have been rendered meaningless. This strongly confirmed our view that the everyday technical operation of all nuclear facilities is highly dangerous.

61. Nationalism Against the Nation State

One powerful manifestation of dissent against the current world system is the existence of a wide variety of movements seeking to revise either boundaries or allegiances. While they are not all necessarily beneficial, they reflect some of the irrationalities in the world's division into states and in some cases suggest that there may be further proliferation (see *Map 2: The Proliferation of States* and the corresponding note).

Separatist movements seek to create a new state out of one or more already established. Irridentist movements seek a readjustment of state frontiers. Regionalist movements seek to achieve some or more autonomy within their established state. We have been forced to make our own judgements about these movements and have coded the information into easily understood shorthand descriptions.

All movements have been classified as either active or dormant. An active movement is one whose activities have evoked a significant response from authority, usually involving police or army action of some kind. A dormant movement is one considered to have been active within the last ten years or so, which may well become active again, but which was not active at the end of the seventies.

Such definitions inevitably encompass wide variations. The separatist movement in Wales, however serious its intentions, is at present little more than a source of irritation to the government of the United Kingdom. Whereas the separatist movements of the Kurds have involved more than one established state in protracted warfare and remain a major source of conflict in the region.

The current armed struggle in Namibia is defined as separatist, since it is primarily directed to ending that country's effective integration with South Africa. But since Namibia has always been a separate territory, whose independence is recognized by the United Nations and its member states, including recently South Africa itself, its struggle is less a manifestation of separatism than a national rebellion against an occupying foreign power.

The government of Taiwan, like the government of China, claims Taiwan to be an integral part of China. In this context, there is a Taiwanese separatist commitment in the Formosan Independence Movement.

We have not attempted to depict the complex situation in the USSR in this map. For this, see *Map 62: Russia's Ununited Republics.*

62. Russia's Ununited Republics

In a state as centralized, diverse and extensive as the USSR, nationalist challenges are inevitable though repressed. Challenge to state control, and to the dominance of the Russian republic within the USSR, date back to the resistance of the Georgian people to incorporation during 1921–22. This event was directly responsible for the conflict between Lenin and Stalin at the end of Lenin's active political life. Stalin won the day and ever since, the Russian government — we use the word 'Russian' advisedly — has reacted with consistent ferocity to crush any movement for or towards national self-determination.

Despite propaganda and education, as well as more brutal methods of repression, nationalist movements have continually emerged, not least among the peoples of the 'annihilated' republics: the five Autonomous Soviet Socialist Republics or ASSRs (Crimean, Chechen-Ingush, Kabardino-Balkar, Kalmyk, and Volga German) and the Karachay Autonomous Region. All of these disappeared from official maps of the Soviet Union in the early years of the second world war and their entire populations were deported to Soviet Central Asia. Four of them (Chechen-Ingush, Kabardino-Balkar and Kalmyk ASSRs and the Karachay AR) were restored in 1957.

Information on resistance movements in the USSR is necessarily scant and uncertain and distinctions between levels of activity must be a matter of judgement. In gathering material for this map, we have called upon a number of experts and a large variety of sources, including oblique references in official reports.

The psychiatric 'hospitals' identified on this map are used for the punishment and control of political dissent. They are administered not by the Ministry of Health but by the Ministry of the Interior.

63. 'Our Bodies Our Selves'

A central theme of the women's liberation movement is the need for women to take charge of their own fates, a right widely denied them by the male-dominated societies of our world. The most satisfactory measure we have found for its success in this respect is contained in this map on abortion rights.

The map shows the spread in legal provisions: from states in which the right to abortion is denied women altogether, to states in which there is some recognition that women should have the right to decide for themselves. In most states there is some right to abortion, but on more or less restricted criteria, and by leave of some, predominantly male, authority.

In no state is the right to abortion a woman's own. Even in the Netherlands, possibly the most liberal in practice, abortion on demand is available only in non-profit clinics; with formal legal sanction for abortion only on narrow medical grounds. In Cuba, another liberal state, abortion on demand is available in government hospitals. Both the Netherlands and Cuba have been put in the most liberal category.

Where abortion is available on demand for certain groups of women only, the criteria differ widely. They include age (usually women over forty); the number of living children (the number varies); and even, in Hungary, whether women have a home of their own. Where abortion is permitted within a specified time limit, that limit is usually the first ten to twelve weeks of pregnancy, as in most of Eastern Europe, but can be as little as eight weeks (Sweden) or as much as twenty-four weeks (Singapore).

Very often, legal provision and social practice are wide apart. France, while fairly liberal in theory, is restrictive in practice; in the Philippines, the opposite is true.

The definitions used need explanation: 'social or social-medical grounds' cover the well-being of the woman and her existing family; 'juridical grounds' cover rape and incest; 'broad medical and eugenic grounds' cover abortion granted to safeguard a woman's physical health and to prevent the transmission of incurable hereditary diseases; 'narrow medical grounds' cover only cases where a woman's life is at stake. We have taken 'social or social-medical grounds' to be a broader category than 'medical, juridical or eugenic grounds' and have adopted it as the determining one where both are given.

In some states with a federal system of government, national legal provisions are moderated by state law and range from extreme liberality (California in the US, Slovenia in Yugoslavia, and South Australia) to extreme restrictiveness (Louisiana in the US, Queensland in Australia).

The inset map shows changing official attitudes to abortion and draws attention to the danger that liberal trends can be reversed where women are not in full control of the decision on abortion. Many East European states, for example, having induced women to enter the labour force by making abortions freely available after the second world war, are now trying to reverse the consequent decline in new entrants to the labour force and the armed services by making abortion more difficult to obtain.

64. The Student Sixties

The student unrest that so spectacularly characterized the closing two years of the sixties was not a new phenomenon. A prominently student opposition to government policy has been endemic in many parts of the world since the second world war; notably in Latin America. Students were in the forefront of the British Campaign for Nuclear Disarmament in the early sixties; were leading militants of the Civil Rights Movement in the United States; and staged, in 1964, on the Berkeley campus of the University of California, a revolt that served as the prototype and pre-cursor of hundreds that took place across the world before the end of the decade.

The student upheavals in each country may be traced to particular conditions or events. In France, it was the sclerotic inflexibility of the Gaullist educational – and political – regime. In West Germany, earlier, in 1967, it was a state visit by the Shah of Iran and the harshness with which his security was protected. In the United States, it was the Vietnam war and the associated demands of the draft. But although there were, everywhere, particular issues and circumstances, there was also a sense of unity that encouraged protest to leap from one campus to another and from one country to another, in a remarkable international movement that was always dramatic and occasionally, as in France and the United States, so important as radically to alter the political scene.

In promoting this sense of unity, an instrument of undoubted influence was the rapid communication of events, by press, radio, and, most vividly, television. But there was too, an underlying unity of dis-content, at educational regimes which processed rather than educated the huge numbers of students resulting from the university expansion of the preceding period, and which provided degrees without acceptable opportunities of employment.

We have defined student disruptions as any student demonstrations that interrupted the normal course of teaching or administration and which led to outside intervention. In a few states, there were disruptions in sites so close together – as at various universities within Tokyo – that they could not be depicted separately on the map. We have identified 89 individual sites in the United States, 37 in Japan, and 32 in Pakistan. Finally, we found no way of singling out sites of repeated student disruption, without causing confusion.

65. Urban Heavings in the Seventies

Urban disorders were no more peculiar to the seventies than student disruptions to the end of the sixties (see *Map 64: The Student Sixties*). But just as student disruption in 1968–69 was remarkable for its extent and its impact, so urban disorder in the seventies reached an unprecedented incidence and intensity.

Some common factors can be identified: both were promoted by improved communications and especially by television; both were prompted by particular incidents, conditions or circumstances in their state of origin; but again, in both there was an underlying unity of impulse, emanating here from increased urbanization (see *Map 50: The Swelling Cities*) alongside a general decline in economic growth. While there was no corresponding increase in employment opportunities (see *Map 55: Industrial Droop* and *Map 52: The Unemployment Time Bomb*), there was an explosive increase in areas of urban deprivation (see *Map 49: Slumland*) accompanied by pressures from inflation (see *Map 56: The First Inflationary Crest, 1974*), especially on the lives of the poor.

An urban upheaval is defined as an urban disorder sufficiently serious in intensity or extent to involve intervention of the authorities by force. Industrial action has been included where it reflects social revolt rather than specific strikes over wages or working conditions. Urban upheavals which have led to a change in government policy or of the government itself are indicated on the site of the national or regional capital.

Subject Index